CONTENTS

PART 2: THE CHARACTER OF MARTIN LUTHER

PART 3: THE LEGACY OF MARTIN LUTHER

ACKNOWLEDGMENTS

*T*HE AMOUNT of scholarship devoted to the life and the thought of Martin Luther is vast and rich. I hardly scratched the surface of it all, but I hope this little book will inspire some readers to delve deeper. So I acknowledge with gratitude all the scholars on whom I depended for this project.

I appreciate too those who encouraged me to delve into that scholarship myself and to explore Luther and his times. I had always wanted to do that, but David Vaughan and Ronald Pitkin, in inviting me to contribute to this series, got me going, to my great enrichment.

Thanks, too, to Paul McCain, who brought me into the project of the edition of the Book of Concord being published by Concordia Publishing House. The chance to work on the Smalcald Articles by Luther and "The Treatise on the Primacy of the Pope" by Philip Melanchthon—including wrestling with their masterful Latin and German and trying to approximate what they said in my far poorer English—helped me to appreciate them even more. At least in my imagination, that project put me in the middle of the tumultuous times in which they confessed their faith.

The historical details cited in this book, except where otherwise noted, are taken from Martin Brecht's magisterial three-volume biography of Luther, which I acknowledge with gratitude.

Thanks, too, to the board members of the Cranach Institute for supporting me in my work: Ilona Kuchta, George Strieter, Todd Peperkorn, David Speers, and Bruce Gee. Thanks, too, to Dean Wenthe, the president of Concordia Theological Seminary. Also to Marvin Olasky of *World Magazine* for giving me the opportunity to write full time.

Above all, I am grateful to my wife, Jackquelyn, whose patience and active support during the very busy months of this writing I appreciate more than words can say. And though I do not compare myself to Luther at all, whenever I read about his love and appreciation for Katie von Bora, I thought of Jackie.

INTRODUCTION

*I*F I had a place to stand," said Archimedes, "I could move the world." The great Greek engineer was referring to the wonders of the lever, that simple yet astonishingly powerful machine whose properties Archimedes was discovering. He realized that, in principle, the capability of the lever was unlimited. An ordinary weakling could move a boulder the size of a house. All he needed was a fulcrum, a pole strong enough so that it would not break and long enough to multiply the force. That, and a place to stand. The force-multiplying physics of the lever are a function of distance. The heavier the object or the weaker the person trying to move it, the longer the pole you would need and the farther away from it you would have to stand. But with the right fulcrum, the right bar, and the right distance, all you would have to do would be to push the lever down, and the boulder, no matter how heavy it was, would move.

Theoretically, with the right fulcrum, bar, and distance, you could put a lever to planet Earth and move the world itself. If, of course, you had a place to stand. That, naturally, is the rub. You can't move the world because you cannot get out of the world. You are in it, so it becomes impossible to step outside the world so as to move it or even change it.

Archimedes did not know about space travel, nor did he realize that the world is moving on its own, though we cannot perceive it. But his point holds, and not just for physics.

Try to change the universe. You can't. You are part of it. You have no place to stand.

Try to change the culture. Social reforms are maddeningly frustrating because the people making the reforms tend to be part of the problem. They themselves have been shaped by the culture they are trying to shape. Even conservatives trying to change the postmodern culture often find that they are conservative in a distinctly postmodern way. They have no place to stand.

Or, for an even more difficult challenge, try to change yourself. The problem is, you *are* yourself. You can work as hard as you can to get rid of that bad habit, that persistent sin. You might make some progress if you have enough willpower. But what if the source of your sin is precisely your will? How can willpower correct the weakness of your will? You have no place to stand.

The Archimedean paradox applies over and over again.[1] It helps to explain the difficulties of leadership: how to move a family, a business, a church, a government. If you are the leader, what if the problem is the leadership? What do you do then? You need a place to stand.

It helps explain the futility of humanism. Why have we not created the perfect world? Why do we still have wars and poverty and cruelty and misery? We all want peace and happiness. So why have we never been able to achieve them? And why do the very schemes to engineer a perfect society, every utopian system and every socialist scheme of economic justice, only make things worse, creating more war and poverty and cruelty and misery? Human beings cannot change themselves. We need a place to stand.

On April 18, 1521, a thirty-seven-year-old monk from a small town in Germany found himself hauled in front of the emperor. The monk had struggled with guilt and futile attempts to improve himself until he started studying the Bible and came to understand what had been all but forgotten in the church of his day: the gospel that our salvation depends not on our works but on the grace of God through the life, death, and resurrection of Jesus Christ. This was such good news to this monk that he started teaching it, which, in turn, required him to teach against the false spiritual system that had kept him and that continued to keep most people in bondage.

Being an academic in a small backwater university, he posted some theses he wanted to debate. He took issue with the way the church was selling indulgences instead of proclaiming the gospel. The sound of his hammer nailing those theses to the church door reverberated far beyond his small town in ways he never anticipated or intended. Before long, the pope of Rome was trying to destroy him. Then the Holy Roman emperor joined the fray.

On that April day it all came to a head. The monk was being tried by the emperor and all his vassals, with the one church through the pope's representatives serving as prosecutor. The monk was all by himself against the ultimate political and spiritual authorities of his day. At the end, it all came down to a very simple question: Will you take back everything you have been teaching about the gospel? Or will you be cast out of the church and state as a heretic and be burned at the stake?

The monk replied that his conscience was bound by the Word of God: "Here I stand."

Martin Luther had a place to stand. And he did move the world. He changed his life. He changed the church. He changed the culture.

At the recent turn of the millennium, a number of publications surveyed experts and the public to determine who were the most influential people of the last thousand years. *Life* magazine ranked Luther number three, after Thomas Edison and Christopher Columbus.[2] The *Toronto Globe & Mail* ranked Luther number two, just after Albert Einstein.[3] Those periodicals were looking for the top hundred, but a more ambitious and possibly more scholarly assessment, in a book ranking the top thousand, placed Luther as number three.[4] Number two was Columbus, and number one was Johannes Gutenberg, hailed as "the man of the millennium" for his printing press, which made possible the information age.

Of course, it was Luther who turned Gutenberg's invention into an engine—consider it a lever—of revolutionary change as his theses and writings were printed and distributed throughout Europe, so that his understanding of the gospel spread like wildfire. Gutenberg is known for printing the Bible, but it was Luther who made the Bible the printing press's biggest seller. He did that by making the Bible central in both theology and the culture, and he made it central in the lives of ordinary people by translating it into a language they could read.

But first the largely illiterate public had to be taught how to read, and Luther was largely responsible for igniting an explosion of education. Luther wanted everyone to be able to stand on the Word of God, so he started schools that would pursue his goal of universal education—bringing literacy not just for a clerical elite but for women, peasants, and everyone. Luther wanted them to read the Bible, but once they could read the Bible, they could read anything. And once the underclasses were educated, class barriers were undermined, former peasants started businesses and became rich, social mobility started to happen, and political freedom and self-government were just a matter of time.

So even secularists admit the influence of Luther in the secular arena. They also credit him for breaking the shackles of the Middle Ages, for a new valuation of marriage and the family, for his doctrine of vocation that created a new work ethic, for the concept of individual thinking, for being the first example of the "modern mind," and for much else.

But he could not have had any of this influence as a mere obscure monk locked in his cloister when he was not teaching his classes at his little university. He was able to exert this influence because he had found a place to stand: the Word of God, which he, in turn, made available in all its liberating power to others. By the Word of God, he meant the Bible, yes, and more specifically the Word of the gospel that he found as he read the Bible. That Word gave him faith in Jesus Christ and in the free gift of salvation that He accomplished on the cross. That faith changed Luther's life—from the outside—and it gave him the freedom and the confidence to face down the world.

That faith also turned Luther, very much against his will, into a leader who had to manage the forces he had unleashed. He was put into the position of having to apply the Word of God to all of life. He had to lead despite overwhelming opposition from seemingly every side. But true, saving faith, Jesus Himself tells us, can move mountains (Matthew 17:20).

Luther moved the world because he had a place to stand. And since we have that same Word, so can we.

CHRONOLOGY

1483	November 10, Martin Luther is born
1501–5	Attends Erfurt University
1505	July 2, the thunderstorm; vows to become a monk. Enters the monastery on July 17.
1510	November, journeys to Rome
1511–12	Transfers to Wittenberg, where he earns his doctorate
1517–18	Sometime in this period, Luther has his "Tower experience," in which, while studying Romans, he understood the gospel.
1517	October 31, posts the Ninety-five Theses
1518	April 26, Heidelberg Disputation
	August, Melanchthon arrives at Wittenberg
1518–19	Controversy, attacks, and counterattacks over Luther's critique of indulgences
1520	June 15, the pope issues his bull against Luther
	October 6, Luther writes *On the Babylonian Captivity of the Church*
	November, Luther writes *On the Freedom of the Christian*
	December 10, Luther burns the pope's bull

A Place to Stand

Part 1

The Life of Martin Luther

I only urged, preached, and declared God's Word, nothing else. And yet while I was asleep, or drinking Wittenberg beer with my Philip Melanchthon and Amsdorf, the Word inflicted greater injury on popery than prince or emperor ever did. I did nothing, the Word did everything.

—Martin Luther

THE MINER'S SON

*H*ANS LUTHER, LIKE MOST people in the late Middle Ages, grew up on a farm. The family was of peasant stock, but unlike most peasants they actually owned their own farm, just a little patch of ground with some cows, sheep, and pigs. Hans was the oldest, but he had the bad luck to live in the province of Thuringia, in Germany, where, under the law, the *youngest* son inherited the property.

So Hans became a miner, taking up the hard, backbreaking work of digging out copper ore. Hans, though, had some ambition. He bought a smelter to process the copper out of the ore. He became a businessman. The price of copper in Germany depended on world markets, and it rose and fell unpredictably. Hans would vacillate from prosperity to destitution all his life. But becoming a businessman gave him something even harder to get and more prized than money in those days: a measure of status. He had never gone to school and never learned to read, but Hans Luther became a member of the middle class, which allowed him to sit on the town council. And he got to marry Margarete Ziegler, the daughter of the richest family in the village of Mohrn, a metropolis of sixty people.

They had eight children, three of whom died at an early age. Their second son was born on November 10, 1483. He was baptized on November 11 and named after the saint who was being commemorated on that day, Saint Martin. This was in Eisleben, a city of more than four thousand. The next year the family moved to Mansfeld, population two thousand, where young Martin Luther would live until he was fourteen.

Hans and Margarete were loving parents, but in the custom of the time, they could be harsh. The church taught that transgressions must be paid for, a notion that was taken up in families, schools, and the legal system. Once, little Martin stole a single nut. He was whipped till he bled. Once, after receiving a severe beating, little Martin withdrew from his father, who then, showing his soft heart, worked hard to win him back. Luther would later criticize harsh punishment for children, but he had no doubt that his parents loved him and he never spoke of them without affection and appreciation.

Hans noticed Martin's giftedness and wanted him to get an education, both for his sake and, no doubt, to advance the family's social standing. When he was seven, Martin went to the little school in Mansfeld, a "trivium" school where he was taught grammar, logic, and rhetoric plus a little music. Here he was taught Latin, the language of all the instruction.

During the Middle Ages all educated people spoke and wrote in Latin. It was the language of all Europe.

Though remnants of the old European tribes persisted so that people of the different regions did have their own culture and language, nations, as we know them, hardly existed at all. Under the feudal system, governments were highly decentralized, with the small principality, not the nation-state, being the main legal unit. But a lord had a lord of his own, as did that lord, and the networks caused by conquest and intermarriage with other powerful families were complex. For generations the English kings had been French, speaking no English and often still living in France. The Holy Roman emperor in Luther's time was Spanish, ruling also Italy and much of Germany.

But because of Latin, there was no language problem. The business of the courts could be transacted and recorded in a common language. A young man from England could study at the University of Paris, enter the service of an Italian duke, and then become a priest in Germany, never encountering a significant language barrier. Everything was in Latin.

So even the lowest and the poorest of schools was a Latin school. At young Martin's first school the curriculum was good, but the teachers, he would recall later, were terrible. Again, you had to pay for your transgressions. Luther recalled getting beaten fifteen times in a single morning for not being able to conjugate and decline some Latin words that he had not learned. The pupil ranking at the bottom of the class wore a wooden jackass around his neck. He could, however, pass it to someone else who was so careless as to lapse into his native German rather than Latin.

The teacher would also appoint one of the pupils to be the "wolf," who would compile a "wolf's list" of those who misbehaved or who slipped and spoke a word of German instead of the required Latin. Their offenses were recorded on a slate. At the end of the week, students on the list were punished for their transgressions. But then the slate would be wiped clean. The next week they each began with a "clean slate," which is where the expression comes from.

Luther would later urge schoolmasters not to depend on beating children to make them learn; rather, they should bring out the delight of learning. Of his time in the school in Mansfeld, he said that he "learned less than nothing despite all the flogging, trembling, anguish, and misery."[1]

But then his father decided to find him a good school. When he was fourteen, young Luther was sent off to Magdeburg, a relatively big city of twenty-five to thirty thousand, along with his friend Hans Reinecke, another smelter's son. The two attended the far-better cathedral school there. They lived with the Brethren of the Common Life, giving Martin his first experience with the life of a monastic community.

After a year, he moved again, to Eisenach (population, four thousand), where he had many relatives. Here, at the parish school operated by Saint George Church, he was blessed by finding, at long last, some really good teachers. Instead of beating and humiliating his students, the rector, Johann Trebonius, would take off his biretta—the scholar's hat—to his pupils, in honor of who they might become.

Years later, Luther would credit his teacher Wigand Güldenapf for finally teaching him correct grammar. He kept in touch with his old teacher throughout his life and said that he deserved all honor. Luther would study at Saint George for four years. Here his academic talents flourished. His teachers agreed that young Martin Luther needed to go to the university.

A CLASSICAL EDUCATION

ARTIN'S FATHER, HANS, WANTED the best for his son and agreed that he should further his education at a university, something few of their social class could ever aspire to. That would be expensive. To get the money to send his son to the university and to support him at his studies, Hans would just work harder. Luther later spoke with gratitude about the "bitter sweat and toil" his father went through to allow him to study at a university.

In 1501 eighteen-year-old Martin began his studies at Erfurt, one of the bigger cities in Germany, with a population of some 20,000, whose university was well regarded, taking in 230 new students every year.

New students were received in a ceremony in which they first had to wear a mask of donkey ears and pig's teeth, which they formally removed upon being accepted into the academic community. This symbolized putting off their animalistic stupidity to become rational human beings.

At the university, everyone wore a different kind of gown, according to the academic degree he held. The students were under semimonastic regulations. They had to swear obedience to the rector, and all the students had to attend church together as a group.

The medieval university had a formidable curriculum. To achieve the first degree, the bachelor of arts, students had to complete a rigorous program in the liberal arts. At Erfurt, this meant studying high-level Latin grammar and high-level logic. (Logic was taught by studying Aristotle and various commentaries on his thought.) High-level rhetoric completed the "trivium," which the students were first introduced to as children and which still provided the conceptual foundation of the university curriculum.

For educational content, the B.A. students studied natural philosophy, the knowledge of the external world that would develop into modern science. Erfurt students studied physics, psychology, and astronomy, using as their texts the foundational treatises, again, of Aristotle.

Students would attend three lectures a day plus work exercises in logic and physics. They also had to attend and respond to disputations of the faculty. These were formal debates that involved argumentation for and against particular *theses* that someone would put forward. (This academic exercise, to put it mildly, would prove important in Luther's later career, when a list of ninety-five theses he would post ended up sparking the Reformation.)

Luther breezed through the bachelor's degree course of study, completing the whole program and passing the required oral examinations in only three semesters, the quickest that was allowed.

He went on for his master of arts degree. The Aristotle-heavy curriculum meant another course of lectures on Aristotle's logic and more natural philosophy, featuring the other scientific writings of Aristotle. It also required six months studying Aristotle's *Metaphysics,* eight months on Aristotle's *Nicomachean Ethics,* six months on Aristotle's *Politics,* and one month on Aristotle's *Economics.*

Everyone basically majored in Aristotle, though there were no majors such as in today's universities, as everyone followed the same program. And for all the limitations of this kind of education, working through Aristotle in such depth did build strong, logical thinkers. (Read some Aristotle—say, the *Nicomachean Ethics*—and you will appreciate how this would be the case.)

But master's students did not just study Aristotle. With their thorough grounding in the first three liberal arts—the trivium of grammar, logic, and rhetoric—they went on to four others, the quadrivium of music, geometry, arithmetic, and astronomy.

The main emphasis of this scholastic-style education was on logic, but the University of Erfurt had a few advocates of the newer approach to the liberal arts that emphasized rhetoric over logic, and the humanities over science. This approach to classical education would soon blossom into what would be known as the Renaissance. These early "humanists" (not to be confused with the "secular humanists" who would come later) offered literary lectures on Cicero, Virgil, and other authors. These were "voluntary," not required, and Luther—who would become an advocate of the Renaissance approach to education—probably attended them.

Master's students attended two or three lectures and two exercise sessions every day. In the course of their studies, they had to attend thirty disputations, those debates over theses, and respond to fifteen, which involved taking one's own position on the question and defending one's reasons. The university operated on the principle that those who study should also teach, so master's students also taught classes for beginning students, something advanced B.A. students also did.

It took Luther only two years to pass his master's examinations, and he was ranked second in his class of seventeen. His father was so proud of his son. Hans even started addressing his educated son Martin using the formal pronoun of respect *ihr* (you), rather than the informal pronoun used to address inferiors, family members, and the closest of friends, *du* (thou). Winning his father's respect must have meant a great deal to Martin, who agreed with his father's wishes to study law.

In the medieval university, after getting bachelor's and master's degrees, then and only then could a student specialize, going into the professional schools of law, medicine, or theology. Luther decided to become a lawyer.

A BOLT OF LIGHTNING

*F*OR ALL OF HIS academic success, Martin Luther was a troubled young man. Today he might be diagnosed as having depression. That would describe the feeling, but it ignores the content, what the feelings were about. He described them as an inner struggle, a spiritual trial, torments of his soul. Imagine feeling the emotions of guilt, fear, anger, and despair all at the same time. That would be an approximation of what this young university student was going through.

Part of this inner torment was a vague but overwhelming sense of guilt. Not that Martin was guilty of the kind of carousing, drunkenness, and womanizing that gave many university students—then as now—a bad reputation. Martin's guilt, when these moods struck him, was more vague and unfocused. He just felt unworthy and unclean. He was afraid of being damned eternally, and although he felt he deserved it, he was angry at a God who would do such a thing.[2]

This was not clinical depression, though, since that malady typically prevents its victims from doing what they need to do. Luther remained very active and productive despite the spiritual misery he was feeling inside.

While going through these spiritual struggles, after he received his master's degree, Luther, for the first time, held in his hands a Bible. It was in the University of Erfurt library. He had never even seen one before.

He had known bits and pieces of the Bible. Psalms were used in devotions, and brief texts from Scripture were read in church. He thought that was all there was in the Bible. He held in his hands a huge book, and it was all new to him. Since only people with a master's degree were allowed to take books out of the library, he took the Bible home with him and read it voraciously, hungrily.

That the medieval church had drifted so far from the Bible was due in large part to the fact there hardly were any. Bibles were expensive. They had to be copied out by hand, and those copies, in turn, were lavishly illuminated with beautiful calligraphy and elaborately crafted artistic designs, often inlaid in gold. Those who illuminated the manuscripts were honoring the sacred texts, but this meant that Bibles were both valuable and rare. The ordinary parish church did not own one.

Most people were illiterate, of course, so they would not be able to read a Bible if they had one. Theologians did pay homage to the authority of the Scriptures, but its truths were taken as bits of data to be systematized and thought through with the help of the logical structures of Aristotle. Faculty members in the school of theology would lecture on the Bible, though mostly by way of scholastic commentaries. The Bible, known only in its Latin translation by Saint Jerome, was not read very much or studied in its own terms.

But this twenty-year-old law student, in his spiritual torments, found a measure of comfort in reading and rereading the Bible, though he did not then completely understand what it was saying.

In June 1505, six months after receiving his master's and taking up the study of law, Luther went home to Mansfeld to visit his parents. Some think the visit was in connection with a rich marriage that his father was trying to arrange for him.

On July 2 Luther was heading back to the university on foot. About four miles outside of Erfurt, he was caught in a thunderstorm. That is a harrowing enough experience, being out in the open in the rain, the wind, and the thunder. Suddenly, right next to him, a bolt of lightning struck. The electricity knocked him to the ground.

To Luther, this was not just a weather-related accident. He had been struggling with his guilt, his doubts, and the dark night of his soul. To him, the storm that was raging all around him was emblematic of the storm in his heart. And to be zapped by lightning was nothing less than the wrath of God.

He vowed then and there to renounce the world and to become a monk.

BROTHER MARTIN

*H*IS FATHER WAS FURIOUS. After all he had gone through to give his son a good education—hauling those rocks, melting that ore, working night and day to raise the money for his schooling—this was the thanks he got? Having a son who was a lawyer would elevate the social status and the economic security of the whole family. Besides, he and Margarete wanted grandchildren! Monks devoted their lives completely to God, which, to them, included never getting married, never having children, and never having the "worldly" concerns of having to make a living. Instead, they would devote themselves completely to prayer.

Hans Luther confronted his son. In becoming a monk against his wishes, Martin was violating the commandment to honor his father and his mother. Hans disowned his son. He stopped using the respectful pronoun *ihr* (you) that he had been using to refer to his son with the master's degree and started again using *du* (thou), as if to a child, as if to take back all his respect.

Later Hans calmed down, put Martin back in his will, and mended the relationship. But he was deeply hurt. He also challenged his son theologically. "How do you know this call you think you have to be a monk came from God?" he asked. "How do you know it wasn't really from the devil?"

The young more-pious-than-thou Martin must have thought his worldly father was persecuting him for his faith. He must have borne the reproaches with self-righteousness. Later in his life, though, he would concede that his father had a point. It was his father who was standing on God's Word—the commandment to honor one's parents—whereas he was putting his trust in an intense experience. Luther would come to distrust anyone who claimed a direct revelation from God—even, presumably, someone who claimed to have been zapped by a divine thunderbolt—considering that the devil indeed can masquerade as an angel of light (2 Corinthians 11:14) and manipulate us through our unstable emotions.

But Martin at the time insisted on joining a monastery because he wanted to save his soul. By entering holy orders, according to the church teaching of the day, he could merit eternal life.

His friends held a farewell party for him. They then, weeping, escorted him to the monastery. When the door shut behind him, they considered that they had lost their friend forever because he had gone out of this world.

There were a number of monasteries in Erfurt that Luther could choose from. Some of them, as far as Luther was concerned, had become too lax. He wanted a conservative one. He picked the Augustinian hermits because they were the strictest monks he could find.

For medieval Christianity, salvation was by works. You had to earn your salvation. As for your sins, you had to pay. But what about forgiveness, grace, Christ dying for our sins? How could there be any kind of Christianity without that?

Medieval Christianity did teach that Christ died for sinners, but this truth was worked together into such a complex system based on Aristotelian logic and institutional bureaucracy that, in practice, the gospel could hardly be found.

It worked something like this: Yes, Christ died for sinners, and in your baptism your sins have been washed away. But that only applies to the penalty for *original* sin. Your inherited sins from Adam have been taken care of, but your own personal sins you have to bear. These can be forgiven too, through the merits of Christ, but only if you remember to confess them orally to a priest so that you can repent of each one and perform an act of penance to make it up. Then you can be forgiven and absolved by the priest. However, that takes care only of the *eternal* punishment that sin deserves. You still have to suffer the *temporal* punishment you have coming.

That will take place after death in purgatory, whose fires will cleanse you after centuries of torment until you are worthy to enter heaven. But you can get out of purgatory too. Since the church has so much merit built up in its bank account of virtues, thanks to all its saints, that merit can be applied to you or your loved ones by means of *indulgences,* a get-out-of-jail-free card the church is authorized to issue that can release a soul, in whole or in part, from purgatory. As for the grace of God, that grace is dispensed by the church. The sacraments are a way of infusing grace into a person so that (1) he or she is enabled to do good works, and (2) his or her good works are purified enough to be acceptable to God. Thus, a medieval theologian could insist that salvation is by grace, though, in practice, this meant salvation by works.

Earning this salvation was much easier and more certain in the monastery, where a conscientious believer could devote all of his attention and make it his full-time job to save his soul. The ordinary people who worked for a living, who married and had children, and who were preoccupied with such "worldly" concerns could also be saved, of course—leaving your lands and money to the church after your death scored a lot of merit, so many did, funding the foundations that supported the monasteries— but if you wanted to follow the "path of perfection," you would become a monk or a nun. Taking the vows of poverty, chastity, and obedience that made you a member of a religious order was considered to be as efficacious as baptism in returning you to a state of innocence. And the intense life of self-denial, confession, prayer, and worship was designed to keep you that way.

There were fifty-two monks in Luther's monastery. They each lived in a cell measuring about ten feet by eight feet. They would fast from food and water for three days at a time. They had to wear their black wool habit and cowl at all times, even when sleeping. The cells were not heated, so as to further mortify the flesh with the cold of winter.

Throughout the day and night, the community worshiped, following the rites for the "canonical hours." This meant getting up at 3:00 a.m. for matins, with prime at 6:00 a.m., terce at 9:00 a.m., sext at noon, nones at 3:00 p.m., vespers at 6:00 p.m., and compline at 9:00 p.m., right before bed.

Those in religious orders—to this day—must "pray the hours," and failure to do so is considered a serious sin. If it is impossible to worship collectively with others, as would be the case with Luther when he was assigned to university duties, you must at least read each service every day. If you miss some, you may make them up by reading them more times on another day. When he became a busy theologian, Luther would devote whole weekends to making up the canonical hours he had missed by reading the rite for the worship service over and over. Later, when his conflict with the pope broke out, he could not shake his sense of obligation—despite his new understanding of the gospel—but he simply had no time. When he realized that he was four months behind in reciting the canonical hours, he finally gave up the practice. But the fact that he kept the habit so long shows how intensely the practice was driven into him as a young monk.

Thrown into this daily routine was a full mass in the morning and the "chapter," which consisted of listening to readings and a weekly group confession of sins. All the monks prostrated themselves on the floor, and beginning with the oldest, confessed how he had broken the monastic rules. These could be "light sins" (being late to a service, reading or singing poorly; "frivolous conduct" such as letting one's eyes wander; restlessness or falling asleep in a service; laughing or making someone else laugh; spilling food; complaining; or breaking the time of silence after compline), to be atoned for by praying a psalm or two. Or the monks might confess to "serious sins" (arguing, lying, gossiping, speaking to a woman, breaking a fast), which would require as penance praying all of the Psalms and fasting for three days. Then there were the "extremely serious sins" (rebellion, impenitence, having secret possessions, and the actual mortal sins, such as sexual sins, stealing, violence, and the like), which did not usually come up in chapter but would be dealt with in private confession.

One popular feature of these group confessions was being able to bring up the infractions of fellow monks. Something like, "Brother Martin may recall the time when he rolled his eyes during supper when the abbot was warning against excessive Bible reading."

Thus, even when there was nothing particularly sinful about the "sins," a consciousness of sin and penitence pervaded the whole atmosphere of the monastery. This may seem almost comical. How were young men shut up in a monastery even able to commit sins? They were physically prevented from being exposed to the temptations of the world. They were not allowed to even look at a woman, in case they might lust after her. Even with this minor rule-breaking, this was surely a holy crowd. But, no. The monastery was a sinful place.

As Luther would later show, sin is not just a matter of what we do. Sin is a matter of what we are.

"They are not skillful considerers of human things, who imagine to remove sin, by removing the matter of sin," said John Milton in a memorable explanation. "Though ye take from a covetous man all his treasures, he has yet one jewel left, ye cannot bereave him of his covetousness. Banish all objects of lust, shut up all youth into the severest discipline that can be exercised in any hermitage, ye cannot make them chaste, that came not thither so."[3]

The sinful nature inside each of us might break out in seemingly petty ways—not in "wandering eyes" or falling asleep during matins, which they probably could not help doing but in those prim, self-righteous accusations of brother monks so as to get them in trouble. There must have been the same cliques, jealousies, and intrigues in the monastery as in any other group of human beings. One is reminded of Robert Browning's poem "Soliloquy of the Spanish Cloister," in which a monk's hatred for a brother monk seethes in frustrated fantasies, including a scheme for making his rival read a text from Galatians that is so hard to interpret he can hardly avoid doing it wrong, becoming a heretic, and getting dragged down to hell.

Conversely, the virtues these monks were counting on were also petty. Though monasteries, no doubt, did nourish Christian piety in some people and sometimes produced a sense of genuine Christian community, nevertheless, Luther would later raise an important question. You in the cloisters are depending on your good works for salvation? But how are your works even good? Who are you helping? God tells us in His Word to love our neighbors. Cannot that be done better out in the world—for example, in the vocations of marriage, parenthood, and the workplace, which you dismiss as being insufficiently spiritual—where we must deal with actual human beings who need our love and service? Good works of any kind are impossible without changing the heart on the inside, which can only happen through faith in Jesus Christ.

This Luther would realize later. Some monks played the system, learning the habits of external conformity and believing that just following the rules would ensure their salvation. This gave them the assurance of salvation despite any sinful thoughts and attitudes, which could be insulated by hypocrisy and self-righteousness. But Brother Martin possessed an extreme spiritual sensitivity and honesty. His spiritual torment—his consciousness of his sinfulness and his sense that nothing he could do could please God—did not go away when he entered the monastery, though he conscientiously obeyed every rule and practiced every mortification. Instead, his spiritual torment grew worse.

FATHER MARTIN

*T*HE MONASTERY NEEDED MORE priests. Wealthy benefactors had set up endowments to pay for masses to be offered up for their souls, so as to cut down their time in purgatory. What with Luther's education and his exemplary performance as a monk, his order decided that he should be ordained as a priest.

Once a priest was ordained, it was the custom to stage a big celebration on the occasion of his first mass, to which Luther invited all of his family and old friends. His father Hans, who still did not approve, nevertheless made the trip to Erfurt, bringing twenty people with him, which must have included not only his immediate family but a raft of relatives and family friends. His old teacher from Saint George showed up. The monastery even allowed his mother, sisters, and other female relatives inside the chapel, such was the happy occasion.

Luther spent the entire night before his big day prostrated in front of the altar, praying, lying on his face, his arms outstretched as on a cross. He was terrified of what he was about to do: preside at Holy Communion.

Luther believed—and would always believe—that the body and blood of Jesus Christ are actually present in the bread and wine of Holy Communion. Later, he would understand this sacrament as the most vivid and powerful and comforting manifestation of the gospel, of Christ giving His broken body and His spilled blood to us in the most personal way for our forgiveness.

But at the time, in the medieval church, the sacrament was seen as a sacrifice in which Christ is offered up again to God. The mass, understood in this way, was seen as a work of the highest merit. The priest was offering up this sacrifice, which could apply merit to both the living and the dead. (This was why laypeople, who did not have the chance for the holy life as the monks did, would pay for masses to be said for themselves or their relatives, even after their death.) To presume to offer such a sacrifice, the priest should himself be pure, at the risk of divine judgment. Luther spent hours in private confession to prepare himself to offer the sacrifice.

Not only that, but according to the doctrine of transubstantiation, the bread would *become* the body of Christ. It would still appear to be bread, on the surface, but its essence would be changed. The freshly minted priest, prostrate on the chapel floor, was terrified at the thought that soon, when he pronounced the words of institution, he would be holding in his hands God Himself. How could he, a sinful human being, bear to have direct, unmediated contact with the holy God?

The next day, all of his family and friends were there, proudly looking on. It was time for Father Martin to conduct the service. As the liturgy moved into the rite of Holy

Communion, Luther started trembling. He started faltering over the words. He whispered to the assisting priest, probably the prior of the monastery, that he could not go on, that he wanted to run away from the altar. He was sternly ordered to continue. Somehow, as his family and friends squirmed in embarrassment, he got through it. Afterward, at the big feast planned in his honor, he attempted to reconcile with his father, who, again, questioned his calling in the ministry and said that the devil was in it.

Though Luther would come to celebrate mass every day, the magnitude of what he was doing continued to lay heavily on him. Not only would he confess all his sins to another priest before he would say mass, at least once he remembered a sin while he was conducting the service. He stopped everything, called over another priest, confessed the sin, received absolution, and then continued the service.

Luther's superiors at the monastery worried about him. The vicar general of the order—that is to say, one of the main leaders of all the Augustinian monasteries—Johann von Staupitz, came to counsel this spiritually troubled, yet talented and pious young priest.

The powerful ruler of electoral Saxony, Frederick the Wise, had brought Staupitz to his capital, the city of Wittenberg, to found a university and to serve as professor of the Bible. Staupitz had been encouraging his fellow monks to read and to study the Bible. Staupitz had also become known for encouraging the Augustinian monks to go back to the founder of their order, Saint Augustine, the early church father who wrote so perceptively about the grace of God.

Luther's Bible reading—he was the only monk in his monastery who read the Bible—attracted the attention of Staupitz, who became his confessor, his counselor, and in a true sense, his pastor, someone who cared for and ministered to his soul. Staupitz told him he did not need to fear Christ as his judge. Christ was his savior. Christ died for him on the cross so that his sins could be completely forgiven. Whenever Luther fell into his dark moods of spiritual hopelessness, he simply needed to trust the promises of Jesus given in God's Word and to cling to them in faith.

For the first time, Luther was hearing the gospel. The example of Staupitz reminds us that even in those days of theological confusion, there were Christians throughout the Middle Ages who did have a living faith in Christ. Though the full magnitude of this gospel did not yet sink in, Luther would later point back to his talks with Staupitz as a turning point in his life.

DOCTOR LUTHER

*S*OON AFTER HE WAS ordained, his superiors—noting that he already had his master's degree and recognizing his unusual gifts—decided that he should go back to the university to study for a doctorate in theology.

Staupitz agreed, thinking academic study would be good for Luther's troubled mind. He reportedly told Luther to go back to get a doctorate so that he would have something to do. Luther objected, saying that his health was not good enough. Still, Staupitz told him, he should do it, telling him that if he died early, the Lord God could use a good adviser.[4]

Pursuing a doctorate would be a big commitment. It would require at least five years of study in scholastic theology, philosophy, and the Bible. He would also have to take part in disputations and conduct lectures himself. He started back at the university there in Erfurt. But Staupitz, who by this time was dean of the theology faculty at the new university at Wittenberg, invited him to fill in for a philosophy teacher. After going back and forth between the two cities, Luther received his degree from Wittenberg and became a doctor of theology.

Wittenberg was a small backwater town of twenty-five hundred inhabitants, but Frederick the Wise wanted to turn it into a worthy capital. Saxony had just been divided between him and his brother, and his half did not have a university. Frederick spared no expense, starting the university in 1502 and bringing in accomplished faculty members, including not just the old-fashioned scholastics but advocates of the new learning—which included Greek, literature, the humanities—that was already beginning to spark the Renaissance.

A key figure in the formation of Wittenberg University was Staupitz. And in 1512 Staupitz resigned his own professorship of the Bible and saw that it was offered to Dr. Luther.

So far Luther had been an obedient child of the church despite his spiritual struggles and his new inklings about Jesus. In this period he started to question the state of the church. It began when he went to Rome.

While still studying for his doctorate, in 1510, Luther was chosen to be one of two delegates from his monastery to go to Rome, where the Augustinians were meeting to work out some disputes within their order. Never having been on such a long journey or seen such a great city, Luther decided to combine business with devotion and turn his trip to the sacred city into a religious pilgrimage.

With his great expectations and high ideals, he was appalled at what he saw in Rome. Brothels catering particularly to churchmen were operating in plain sight. The rationalization was that the vow of celibacy meant they would not get married, so using prostitutes did not count.

(A mind-set that made marriage something bad but fornication something good.)

When he went to church, the priests were speed-reading through the mass without paying any attention to what they were saying, repeating the words so fast that no one could understand them. Luther tried to find a priest to counsel with and to hear his confession, but the only ones he could find seemed completely uneducated and ignorant, with little respect for the liturgy or the sacraments.

The cardinals, though—the elite bishops clad in scarlet—lived in ostentatious wealth and decadent luxury. He also heard about the open immorality of the recent popes, especially the recently deceased Alexander VI, with his mistresses, his eight illegitimate children, his financial corruption, and his murders.

Luther did the pilgrim tourist routines, visiting the shrines and collecting the indulgences they promised. He would say later he did so many pious deeds he almost regretted that his father and mother were still alive, since he could have freed them from purgatory. It was said that a priest who performed a mass at the church of Saint John Lateran would ensure his mother's salvation. Luther tried to do it, but the crowds were so great he could not get in. He did ascend the church's stairs on his knees, saying the Lord's Prayer on each one, an act of devotion that was said to redeem a soul from purgatory. Luther did it for the sake of his late grandfather. But when he came to the top of the stairs, the thought flashed through his mind, *Who knows whether it is true?*

He left Rome disillusioned, but he tried to turn the experience into motivation: to see so many abuses even in the Holy City, he reasoned, should make him increase his own personal efforts to live a life of good works.

When Luther accepted the call to join the faculty at Wittenberg, he was transferred to the Augustinian monastery there. His mentor, Staupitz, not only stepped down from his professorship so that Luther could have it, he saw that Luther was made subprior of the monastery and its official preacher. Could the gentle, saintly Staupitz have seen that Luther might be the one, more suited than himself, to bring the gospel to his order, to the university, and to the church as a whole?

As Luther took up his duties as professor, he matured into a true theologian, one who was beginning to understand the nature both of human sin and of God's grace. A doctor of theology at that time had considerable authority in expounding the theology of the church. Luther embarked on a series of lectures on the Psalms, Romans, Galatians, and Hebrews.

He argued that the Bible, not the Aristotelian philosophy of the scholastics, was the true source of theology. He taught that our works and rules do not save us, but that we need to understand with the deepest humility where we stand before God as sinful creatures and then know the Christ who shares our sufferings and who changes our inmost attitudes. (This was close, but it was not yet the full gospel that he would discover. His focus in these early years of his teaching was salvation not by works but by our *inner attitudes* and not yet on the objective work of Christ on the cross.)

In his lectures he criticized the corruption and abuses of the church. He urged that his students rediscover Augustine. He spoke out against the superstitious veneration of the saints. His classrooms were packed. The influence of his teaching spread among the students, then among his colleagues. One professor, Andreas Karlstadt, started as a harsh critic, but then was won over by Luther's emphasis on the Bible, though tragically he would later become a harsh critic again, though for very different reasons.

With Luther's assignment to fill the pulpit during services at the monastery, he also developed into a great preacher. At a time when sermons had been reduced to little more than a brief moralistic homily or eliminated altogether in services, Luther realized the overarching importance of preaching the Word of God. Luther preached from Scripture and, speaking from his own personal experience of the struggles of faith, his words struck a chord with others who were also desperate to find a gracious God. When he was preaching, people packed into the chapel to hear him.

In 1517 Luther composed a set of *Theses Against Scholastic Theology,* attacking the reliance on Aristotle and on human reason in favor of a theology based upon Scripture alone. The theses further argued that people could not save themselves by any of their natural powers, that they needed the grace of God. Though still thinking in terms of salvation by works, he proposed a distinction between "works of the law" and "works of grace." He defended these theses in a disputation, then, hoping to spur further debate throughout the academic world, he sent copies to other universities and to other theologians, including John Eck, a papal functionary. The stage was set. But one more thing had to happen.

THE FULCRUM

*L*UTHER WAS WORKING ON a series of lectures on Paul's letter to the Romans. Reading and rereading the epistle in his study in the monastery's tower5—as he was wrestling, as usual, with his own spiritual anguish—a verse that he had been struggling over, trying to understand, suddenly became clear. He described the moment:

> Though I lived as a monk without reproach, I felt that I was a sinner before God with an extremely disturbed conscience. I could not believe that he was placated by my satisfaction. I did not love, yes, I hated the righteous God who punishes sinners, and secretly, if not blasphemously, certainly murmuring greatly, I was angry with God, and said, "As if, indeed, it is not enough, that miserable sinners, eternally lost through original sin, are crushed by every kind of calamity by the law of the Decalogue, without having God add pain to pain by the gospel and also by the gospel threatening us with his righteous-

ness and wrath!" Thus I raged with a fierce and troubled conscience. Nevertheless, I beat importunately upon Paul at that place, most ardently desiring to know what St. Paul wanted.[6]

Notice his honesty: he "hated" God. Luther had done everything he could as a monk to live a life of virtue and to merit salvation, but it was never enough. In going through the Bible, he saw the burden of original sin from Adam, then the challenge of keeping the Ten Commandments, and then, in the New Testament, there were even harder demands, as in the Beatitudes, affecting not just outward behavior but inner attitudes that seemed beyond his control. And now Paul . . . what does *he* want us to do? It seemed so unfair of God to expect what we are not capable of performing. But then, as Luther pondered Romans 1:17, the full meaning of the gospel came to him:

At last by the mercy of God, meditating day and night, I gave heed to the context of the words, namely, "In it the righteousness of God is revealed, as it is written, 'He who through faith is righteous shall live.'" There I began to understand that the righteousness of God is that by which the righteous lives by a gift of God, namely by faith. And this is the meaning: the righteousness of God is revealed by the gospel, namely the passive righteousness with which the merciful God justifies us by faith, as it is written, "He who through faith is righteous shall live." Here I felt that I was altogether born again and had entered paradise itself through open gates.[7]

Luther realized that the issue was not *his* righteousness but *Christ's* righteousness. Yes, all are sinners, and Christ alone lived the perfect life. But Christ's righteousness is credited to *us* when we have faith in Him. Not only that, our sins are credited to Christ, who on the cross bore the punishment that we deserve. Our righteousness is "passive," that is, it is something we *receive* from God in the gift of faith. Salvation is God's action, not our own.

Thus, our salvation is *outside ourselves.* It is to be found in Jesus Christ, in His life, death, and resurrection. When we are connected to Him by faith—which happens as the Holy Spirit works in our heart through the Word and the sacraments—our sins are imputed to Him, and His righteousness is imputed to us. All the works that Jesus did, all His healings and miracles and love, are counted as if we had done them. And all our wretched, embarrassing, vicious sins, Jesus claims for Himself and atones for on the cross. When God judges us, He sees Jesus.[8]

Luther realized that the state of his own pathetic emotions was not so important. Jesus died for him. So what if he struggled with a sense of his own inadequacy before God? Of course he is inadequate before God. But Jesus died for him.

Luther realized that he was saved neither by his works (which he had already realized by now), nor by his attitudes, but by Christ. He further found, though, that this realization of God's love for him in Christ *did* change his attitudes and *did* change his works.

When he was doing good works in order to merit salvation, he was doing them with an ulterior motive that took away their very virtue since he was doing them, really, for himself, thinking that he would be paid back for his good works by the rewards of heaven. Now that he loved God, he found himself loving his neighbors. They too were loved by God, even though they might not deserve it any more than he did. They too have been redeemed by Christ, if they would just stop depending on themselves and receive His grace. He found himself now loving and serving his neighbors spontaneously, not out of external obligation, but because he had been changed from the inside by the miracle of faith.

Luther described how that one verse—"the righteous shall live by faith"—made all of Scripture come together for him. This would be the insight around which all his theology and all his leadership would be built. And the confidence it gave him, the assurance of his salvation and his conviction that God was acting in his life and in the course of the world, gave Luther the courage to overcome the enormous obstacles that he would soon face.

When Luther realized that salvation, grounded in the sacrifice of Jesus and revealed objectively in the Word of God, was outside himself, he finally had a place to stand. We began this book with the paradox of Archimedes, who said, thinking of levers, that he could move the world if he had a place to stand. Luther's biographer, Martin Brecht, in talking about Luther's discovery of the objectivity of the gospel, uses the same metaphor:

This new certainty of forgiveness which comes through the word, something which Luther did not previously have, was simultaneously for him the Archimedian point from which he could conquer his own *Anfechtun-gen* [spiritual struggles], and from which he was also able to move the entire traditional system of repentance off its hinges.[9]

Scholars debate the exact time of Luther's "tower experience." Many assume that it must have happened before the controversy over indulgences broke out. Brecht finds good evidence, though, to date the event as happening sometime in 1518, which would be *after* Luther posted the Ninety-five Theses. "Right in the middle of the indulgence controversy," Brecht says, "Luther had found *a place on which he could stand* in the difficult conflicts ahead of him, and on the basis of which he could develop a new theory and practice of the church."[10]

HEAVEN FOR SALE

*O*N THE CEILING OF the Sistine Chapel in St. Peter's Basilica in Rome is one of the greatest artworks of Western civilization. The great Michelangelo di Lodovico Buonarroti painted a monumental masterpiece depicting the Creation—with the unforgettable image of the hand of God and the hand of Adam reaching out to each other—and other great events of biblical history culminating in the Last Judgment and the end of time.

To this day many marvel at the beauty and sublimity of this work. Tourists cannot say enough about it. They appreciate, too, St. Peter's Basilica itself, the pope's special place of worship and an architectural wonder. In fact, much of the Vatican is an architectural wonder, with masterpieces of Renaissance art and design cramming its every corner.

Most tourists, though, do not realize why all of this art is there, much less how it was paid for. And few realize that all of this aesthetic magnificence precipitated the Protestant Reformation.

Often overlooked is that the money Michelangelo was paid to paint the Sistine Chapel came indirectly from the sale of the very indulgences that provoked Luther into posting his Ninety-five Theses.

Pope Leo X—like Julius II, under whom Michelangelo began his work—was a great fan of Renaissance art. And both popes shared a grand vision of restoring Rome's magnificence. The city had fallen into disrepair over the centuries, thanks in part to the degradation of some of the previous pontiffs. Leo wanted, above all, to finish the cathedral so it would be suitable for the successor to the throne of Saint Peter, the vicar of Christ on earth. And he also had to pay off the debt amassed by Julius, who had started the project. That required cash.

One of the major financial abuses of the church at that time was that church offices were put up for sale. Technically, this was called *simony,* after the sorcerer in the book of Acts who thought he could buy the Holy Spirit for money (Acts 8:9–24). Moralists such as Dante, who devoted one of his levels of hell to popes and other church officials who were guilty of this vice, condemned the practice, but simony had become the recognized way of doing business for years. If you wanted to be a bishop, you had to pay the pope for the appointment. Bishops themselves typically ruled large estates and also controlled lesser offices that they could sell.

One of the most valuable bits of ecclesiastical merchandise was the archdiocese of Mainz, the largest in Christendom, which included vast lands, the leadership of the church in Germany, and the right to help elect the emperor. A young nobleman, Albrecht of Brandenburg, put in for the office. Since he was only twenty-four, he also needed a dispensation from the pope suspending the normal requirements for such a high office. The pope's price: twenty-nine thousand gulden. Albrecht could not come up with that sum, so he and the pope struck a deal. He arranged to borrow the money from the wealthy Fugger family of Augsburg. If the pope would proclaim an indulgence sale in Albrecht's domain in Germany, half of the proceeds would be used to pay off the loan and the other half would go straight to the Vatican. It was a win-win-win situation for Albrecht, the Fuggers, and especially the pope, who would make money both from Albrecht and from the indulgences, giving him plenty of money to pay off the loan that funded Michelangelo and purchased all that marble.

On March 31, 1515, Pope Leo X issued a bull (that is, an official papal pronouncement) for the Indulgence of Saint Peter. It offered "Four Chief Graces":

(1) Complete remission of all sins (on the condition of contrition, confession, a visit to seven churches, and a monetary payment)

(2) Obtaining a letter that would entitle the bearer to receive total absolution twice, anytime he chose, including at the hour of his death

(3) The buyer and all his relatives could have access to all the church's good works, even without confession

(4) Remission of sins for souls in purgatory if someone were to buy them an indulgence.

The price for indulgences was based on a sliding scale that took into account one's social status, vocation, and annual income:

> royalty, twenty-five gulden
> high nobility, ten gulden
> lesser nobility, six gulden
> townsfolk and merchants, three gulden
> artisans, one gulden
> others, half gulden

What a deal! A gulden was a week's wages for a soldier.[11] An artisan, such as a cobbler or a carpenter, could give a week's pay and get all eternity in return. That would take some belt-tightening, but could there be a better rate of return: a week for eternity? A peasant could pay half a gulden and get out of having to live through centuries of purgatory. If he could raise another half gulden, he could free his dead child.

What made the deal even more attractive was that it offered a measure of certainty the church normally refused to give. In the atmosphere of sin counting, no one could be sure he would be saved at all, and then the prospect of suffering for your sins in purgatory for an indefinite period of time, perhaps as much as thousands of years, even if you were saved, put a further damper on life. And if you were a sensitive soul (as Luther was), any kind of assurance of salvation would be worth any price. Half a gulden or twenty-five gulden must have been seen as an incredible bargain, a small price to pay, literally, for eternal life in heaven.

To protect the market, the pope's decree said that all other sermons should be suspended so that the indulgence could be preached at least three times a week. The offer would be good for eight years, the time-period allotted for the sale, and the indulgences could only be purchased in the provinces of Mainz, Magdeburg, and Brandenburg (all of which were Albrecht's domains—of course, the public knew nothing of their new archbishop's financial arrangement with the pope).

A monk named John Tetzel was put in charge of the sale. He was a doctor of theology with experience as an inquisitor of heretics, and he had sold indulgences in other jurisdictions. Like other successful pitchmen, he had the common touch and was a good communicator. He traveled throughout the regions, speaking in churches and in village squares. "Have mercy upon your dead parents," he would say. "Whoever has an indulgence has salvation; anything else is of no avail."[12] "These indulgences have so much power that they would even give you forgiveness if you raped the Virgin Mary."[13] And crowds of desperate, untaught people from all walks of life, some of them poverty-stricken who needed their half gulden to feed their families, bought the indulgences.

These indulgences were not being sold in Luther's Saxony, which was not one of Albrecht's territories, but Saxons were traveling to the three provinces to take advantage of the sale. When Luther heard what Tetzel was saying and doing to sell indulgences, he was shocked. He wrote a letter about these flagrant abuses to the church authorities (whom he assumed had no idea of what was going on), naively addressing the letter to none other than Archbishop Albrecht.

Luther's next step was to propose an academic disputation on the subject.

Indulgences got their start with the Crusades of some centuries earlier. The popes promised that those who would join the campaign to free the Holy Land from the Muslims would receive an indulgence that would free their souls from purgatory. If they died while fighting in this holy war, their souls would go straight to heaven. The result was a sort of Christian jihad, complete with instant paradise for the martyrs who died while fighting the infidel, exactly equivalent to what today's Islamist terrorists believe.

At the time, though, the indulgences were an act of the church to reward those devoted to its cause. Indulgences were then promised for veneration of relics, pilgrimages, and other acts of devotion (as Luther himself, before his awakening, took advantage of in Rome). Giving an offering, of course, could also be a form of devotion. The actual sale of indulgences was a natural development, and it was not uncommon during the late Middle Ages.

Luther composed ninety-five theses about indulgences that he was prepared to argue. These were not dispassionate debating points, though. Thesis by thesis, insight by insight, he dismantled the theological rationalization for indulgences, exposed the corruption of those who sold them, and opened up an alternative vision of what the Christian faith is really all about.

THE WORD NAILED TO THE CHURCH DOOR

*O*N OCTOBER 31, 1517, Luther nailed his Ninety-five Theses to the door of the Castle Church in Wittenberg. Such was the way of posting notices of disputations and other events in those days. But the symbolism is significant. In a time when the church had drifted far away from the Word of God, Luther nailed biblical truth back on to the church.

> THESIS 1. When our Lord and Master, Jesus Christ, said "Repent," He called for the entire life of believers to be one of penitence.[14]

Sin is not something that can be bought off. The Christian must live all of life in a spirit of repentance before God. Indulgences, like the whole penitential system of ritual paybacks, turned the Christian life into a mechanical routine rather than a personal faith.

This first thesis focuses on repentance rather than faith—the theological use of the law, which makes us see ourselves as sinners in need of salvation, rather than the gospel, which makes us see our salvation in the work of Jesus Christ. This is why Martin Brecht dates Luther's evangelical awakening as happening *after* he posted the Ninety-five Theses. By the end of the year, Luther's attacks on indulgences would center on how they detracted from the gospel and how they demanded money for the forgiveness Christ offers as a free gift.

But the first of the theses, the words that began the Reformation, would resonate throughout Luther's future thought. Repentance is for the whole life of the Christian, and so is the other side of the coin: faith in the promises of the gospel. The law and the gospel are not *only* for the beginning of the Christian life, for conversion, but for all of life, bringing grace and forgiveness and strength for everything a Christian might face.

Other theses exposed the blasphemous sales spiels that Tetzel and his sales teams were foisting on the public:

> THESIS 27. There is no divine authority for preaching that the soul flies out of purgatory immediately after the money clinks in the bottom of the chest.[15]

> THESIS 28. It is certainly possible that when the money clinks in the bottom of the chest, avarice and greed increase; but when the church offers intercession, all depends on the will of God.[16]

> THESIS 75. It is foolish to think that papal indulgences have so much power that they can absolve a man even if he has done the impossible and violated the mother of God.[17]

The theological justification for the indulgences was that the church had accumulated a vast "treasure" of merit consisting of the accumulated good works of the saints, who were so virtuous that they had far more merit than they needed, so that the extra could be applied by the pope to whomever he pleased. The theses set up a point-by-point argument dismantling this view, culminating in the obvious question: If the pope really does have the power to apply this treasury of merits so as to let people out of purgatory, why doesn't he, out of sheer love, just let everybody out? Why is he taking money for it?

Luther also was bothered by the way indulgence hawkers were taking hard-earned money from poverty-stricken peasants who needed it to take care of themselves and their families.

> THESIS 46. Christians should be taught that, unless they have more than they need, they are bound to retain what is necessary for the upkeep of their home, and should in no way squander it on indulgences.[18]

The theses show the beginnings of what would later become notorious in Luther's way of arguing: his bold attacks on his opponents, his take-no-prisoners attitude, and his down-to-earth style, all combined with a sharp wit and a devastating sense of humor:

> THESIS 50. Christians should be taught that, if the pope knew the exactions of his indulgence-preachers, he would rather the church of St. Peter were reduced to ashes than be built with the skin, flesh, and bones of his sheep.

> THESIS 51. Christians should be taught that the pope
> would be willing, as he ought if necessity should arise, to
> sell the church of St. Peter, and give, too, his own money
> to many of those from whom the pardon-merchants con-
> jure money.[19]

Though comments like that must have stung, Luther
did not challenge the authority of the pope. Nor did he reject purgatory. (Both would come later.) Luther did not
even reject indulgences of a certain type, saying that the
pope has the authority to remit temporal penalties for vio-
lations of the laws he himself has passed. (For example, to
use a hypothetical case of our own, if the pope decreed
that no one should eat meat on Fridays on pain of impris-
onment, but then granted an indulgence to let some
meat-eaters go free, that would be within his rights. If
someone were to pay for the privilege of eating meat on
Friday, Luther would not be overly bothered.)

But what Luther objected to was the pope's extending
his authority into the realm of the afterlife, the selling of
indulgences as a ticket to heaven, and the obvious financial corruption this entailed. More deeply, the theology of
indulgences was an exaggerated and bureaucratic system
of salvation by merit in direct opposition to the gospel that
Luther himself was just beginning to understand. And yet
the theses already pointed in the direction of where salvation truly was to be found:

> THESIS 36. Any Christian whatsoever, who is truly re-
> pentant, enjoys plenary remission from penalty and guilt,
> and this is given him without letters of indulgence.

THESIS 37. Any true Christian whatsoever, living or dead, participates in all the benefits of Christ and the Church; and this participation is granted to him by God without letters of indulgence.[20]

THESIS 62. The true treasure of the church is the holy gospel of the glory and grace of God.[21]

Luther's proposal for the disputation included the invitation that if anyone could not participate orally, he could do so by writing. But no one took up the challenge to debate his theses. Probably none of Luther's colleagues at Wittenberg wanted to take him on. Besides, the formulation of the theses made them very hard to argue for the contrary position. (Was someone going to argue that an indulgence *could* free someone from the guilt of raping the Virgin Mary? Was someone going to take the position that the pope *should* build St. Peter's on the flesh and bones of the peasants whom Tetzel was swindling?) Luther was disappointed that he had no takers. So he sent copies of his theses to other universities and theologians.

Although there was no Internet in 1517, the information technology that would later develop into the Internet had already had its beginning. The printing press had just been invented by Johannes Gutenberg in 1450, and with Luther's Ninety-five Theses, the media had its first major, culture-changing impact. In Wittenberg the theses circulated only in handwritten copies. Then someone took a copy to Nuremberg, where they were printed in mass quantities. A print shop in Leipzig printed even more. Then a printer in Basel, Switzerland, spread them in that country. The theses, of course, were in Latin, so they were comprehensible all over Europe. Someone translated them into German so they also circulated among the common people.

They created a sensation. The great artist Albrecht Dürer read them and was so impressed and grateful for the insight that he sent Luther a gift. Desiderius Erasmus, the Renaissance sage, read them and sent a copy to his friend Thomas More in England.

The panicky Albrecht, the new archbishop of Mainz, sent them to Pope Leo X, who was not amused. He tried to get the Augustinian order to shut up their monk. He brought in Vatican theologian John Eck to respond to Luther's theses. Eck wrote a book against Luther, citing the scholastic theologians as his authorities. Luther wrote a book against Eck, citing the Bible as his authority. An all-out polemical war broke out. Tetzel wrote pro-indulgence theses that were debated at the University of Frankfurt. When copies were brought to Wittenberg, the students burned them.

Luther let no attack on him and his positions go unanswered, getting more forceful every time. "From then on," according to Brecht, "Luther the polemicist is characterized by frank outrage against his opponents, not infrequently also by classical imagery and formulations from the humanists, and last but not least by his own humor and powerful language."[22]

The younger generation especially seized on Luther's words. So did laypeople tired of being bilked and robbed by their own church. Thoughtful people had long believed the sale of indulgences was a scam—see Geoffrey

Chaucer's "Pardoner's Tale" written two centuries earlier—but Luther dared to say what everyone else was afraid to, and he undermined the very foundations of the church's rickety rationalizations.

Tetzel, an inquisitor as well as an indulgence salesman, was not worried. "In three weeks," he said, "I will throw the heretic in the fire."[23]

FREDERICK THE WISE

*E*UROPEAN GOVERNMENTS IN THE Middle Ages were based on elaborate hierarchies of authority—with minor nobles owing allegiance to greater lords, who might owe allegiance to kings, who might owe allegiance to the emperor. Yet, in many ways, the feudal system was a highly decentralized form of government, with local rulers often having precedence over any kind of central authority. Government in the Middle Ages also put great emphasis on "rights." Every step of the social and political hierarchy—the peasants, the city-dwelling middle class, the minor nobility, the ruling princes—had their rights, which could not be taken away even by their superiors. Each had their spheres of authority that the other spheres were to respect.

Absolute monarchs—rulers who admitted no limits to their authority and whose will was law—were an invention of humanism. Louis XIV, the Enlightenment-era "Sun King," was vastly more powerful as the king of France than the medieval Louis IX, canonized as a saint. M. Stanton Evans, in his book *The Theme Is Freedom: Religion,*

Politics, and the American Tradition, documents how Christianity from the very beginning influenced its culture in the direction of freedom and limited government. By contrast, it was the legacy of humanism that gave human beings absolute power.[24]

There were no nation-states in Luther's day, and Germany did not even have a king. Different "princes" ruled the various provinces—not sons of kings, as in our more familiar definition of the term—but dukes, margraves, counts, and even bishops who ruled "principalities." These princes, though, did have a feudal lord, the Holy Roman emperor.

The Roman Empire, of course, was long gone, but Charlemagne, the French king who brought Europe out of the dark ages of the barbarian tribes, was given the title of emperor by the pope. After his death, Charlemagne's domains split, with the kingdom of France separating from what would become the empire. The Holy Roman Empire included several hundred principalities in what is now Germany, Austria, Switzerland, Belgium, the Netherlands, Czechoslovakia, western Poland, and northern Italy. When Charles V was made emperor, he was already the king of Spain, bringing in not only Spain but the Spanish holdings in South and Central America.

The empire even had a legislature, the diet. This was composed of all the princes of the various principalities, who met periodically with the emperor to agree on laws and to deliberate on common problems.

And although the Holy Roman Empire was far from a democracy, the emperor was chosen by an election. Only seven princes, though, got to vote: three bishops and four laymen. These "electors" were especially powerful and enjoyed special prerogatives, equivalent to those of kings. One of the electors happened to be the ruler of Saxony, Frederick the Wise, one of whose subjects was Martin Luther.

The church at that time did not depend on voluntary offerings—contributions to the church were mandatory, amounting to a tax that burdened peasants and lords alike. Many of the princes greatly resented the way the church was plundering their realms, and the sale of indulgences was just another drain on their already shaky economies. They also resented the way the pope kept playing politics, insisting that he held the ultimate authority not only over the spiritual realm but over earthly realms as well, acting out these claims by waging wars and seizing territories.

Elector Frederick agreed, though in many ways he embraced the conventional piety of the day. For example, he owned one of the biggest collections of relics—bones of saints and alleged souvenirs of biblical figures (Mary's veil, a piece of sail from Peter's ship, a nail from the cross)—the veneration of which had indulgences tied to them. Not wanting the competition from Tetzel was one reason Elector Frederick forbade the sale of Saint Peter's indulgences in his realm.

But Frederick had a court chaplain and adviser named George Spalatin who embraced Luther's teachings and became one of his closest friends. And Frederick was proud of his university and of this professor who was making a name for himself. Also, he seems to have been a good ruler who believed that part of his calling was to protect his subjects.

In June 1517 charges were filed against Luther in Rome. He was to appear within sixty days or face the "ban," which entailed not only excommunication, expelling him from the church and its sacraments, but forbade anyone from giving him shelter or protection, making him an outlaw who could be killed on sight.

The charges against Luther were that he denied the authority of the pope. Ultimately, the only argument for indulgences was that the pope said they were valid, and Luther's insistence on judging theology by Scripture threatened the pope's whole reign.

Luther knew that if he went to Rome, he would be condemned and very likely burned at the stake, as had happened with others in the Middle Ages who questioned the papacy in the name of the Bible and the gospel, such as the Czech Jan Hus, who had been burned a hundred years earlier. Technically, the church could not execute anyone. Rather the church could put someone under the "ban" and then turn the heretic over to "the secular arm," to an earthly ruler who could exact the death penalty. This is why the church needed the cooperation of someone like the emperor to put down heresy.

Luther confided his fears to Spalatin, who interceded for him with the elector. Frederick demanded that Luther be tried not in Rome but in Germany.

The pope did not want to alienate Elector Frederick. After all, the current emperor, Maximilian, was getting old, and a new election would come soon. The pope wanted his ally, the king of France, to be given the empire, and he definitely did not want the election to fall on young Charles, Maximilian's grandson, the king of Spain. So the pope agreed to send Cardinal Tommaso Cajetan to the diet meeting in Augsburg to hear Luther's case. But this was to be no trial. Cajetan would allow Luther to recant everything he had been teaching. Otherwise, he would be put under the ban as a heretic.

Cajetan promised Elector Frederick that he would not make Luther a prisoner. The elector paid Luther's expenses to the diet and gave him some legal advisers. And Staupitz came to support him.

Luther went to Augsburg, aware of the threat. He wrote to his friends, "Let Christ live, let Martin die."[25]

He was instructed to fall on his face before Cajetan. He did. Cajetan interrogated him on two points: on his objections to the treasury of merit in indulgences as a denial of the authority of the pope and on his new understanding of justification, that a person could be assured of salvation. (The official position was that justification was a human work, and so it was uncertain; Luther believed justification was the work of God and therefore certain.) Thus Cajetan cut to the heart of the real issues: the authority of Scripture and the sufficiency of the gospel.

The cardinal started shouting. Luther asked for time to collect his thoughts. That night he composed a reply, affirming his trust in the Bible and in the gospel and asking that Cajetan show from the Bible where he was wrong.

When they met, though Luther was not supposed to dispute his case, simply decide whether or not he would recant, they started arguing. Cajetan told Luther to get out and not to come back unless he was going to recant. Stalling, Luther filed an appeal with the pope.

Staupitz, aware that the pope was putting pressure on the Augustinian order to rein in their monk, absolved Luther of his vow of obedience so that he would not have to respond to his monastic superiors' instructions to shut up.

On October 20, 1518, Luther snuck out of Augsburg in the middle of the night. The city gates were closed, so friends smuggled him out, not by letting him down in a basket as friends had done with the apostle Paul (Acts 9:25), but by slipping him through a small gate through the wall. A horse was ready for him, and he rode nonstop for Saxony.

Rome turned to diplomacy to get Elector Frederick to turn over Luther. The pope sent him the Golden Rose of Virtue, a gilded flower signifying the pope's greatest favor, trying to flatter the elector into going along with his wishes. He sent a different papal representative, Karl von Miltitz, to soften his position. Von Miltitz criticized the excesses of Tetzel and tried to strike a compromise.

But then, in the midst of the diplomacy and the pope's efforts to get Luther, on January 12, 1519, Emperor Maximilian died. By imperial law, the elector of Saxony, along with the elector of the Palatinate, served as vicars to rule the empire until a new emperor could be elected.

For now, Frederick was coruler of the empire. The pope needed his vote for his candidate, the king of France. He did not want Frederick to vote for King Charles of Spain. So the pope backed off. The issue of Martin Luther had to be tabled.

WILD BOAR IN THE VINEYARD

*O*N JUNE 28, 1519, the seven electors convened and chose Charles I of Spain, who became Charles V, emperor of the Holy Roman Empire.

This was not who the pope wanted. But now there was no reason for the pope not to act against both Luther and his theology. On July 24, 1520, he issued a bull entitled *Exsurge Domine* for its opening words, "Arise, O Lord," going on to call upon Him to act against the "wild boar" who was destroying the Lord's vineyard.

The proclamation listed forty-one statements found in Luther's writings (without mentioning any titles). The document stated that *anyone* who held these views was to be condemned. As for Luther, he was forbidden to preach, his books must be burned, and he must send a recantation to Rome. If not, he and his followers would be declared heretics.

Luther was given sixty days. After that, if he had not taken back his teachings, he was to be excommunicated. No one would be allowed to associate with him. Any legal authority was obliged to seize him and send him to Rome. Anyone who sheltered him would also be condemned.

The bull was to be published and distributed by Luther's opponent John Eck so that Luther and everyone else would be aware of the papal pronouncement. Eck was also to give a copy to the new emperor, who was to arrest Luther and carry out the book burnings.

Frederick the Wise was informed that he, too, and his whole family would be excommunicated if he continued to protect Luther. Spalatin urged Frederick to win the emperor to Luther's cause. Luther filed an appeal to the new emperor, an inexperienced young man who was only nineteen years old.

But the emperor had already received the bull. And he had already arranged for Luther's books to be burned throughout his realm.

When the papal bull arrived in Wittenberg, the whole university turned out to watch Luther burn it.

So on January 3, 1521, a bull of excommunication was issued against Luther and his protectors.

Frederick wrote to the pope, insisting that Luther must be refuted first, shown why he was wrong, and given a fair trial. He asked the emperor to hear him at the upcoming diet to be held at Worms.

Several of Luther's followers wanted to take up arms against Rome, but Luther forbade it. Not by the sword, he said, but "by the Word only will the church be preserved."[26] Instead Luther responded with another book, this one entitled *Against the Execrable Bull of the Antichrist.* A wild boar, indeed.

The Theologian
of the Cross

*W*HILE ALL OF THIS was going on, Luther's
understanding of the gospel was maturing
and deepening, and he began to see its implications for
the entire church.

Six months after he posted his theses, in April 1518, the
Augustinians were holding a general meeting at Heidelberg. Staupitz asked Luther to present something on his
new evangelical insights unrelated to the indulgence controversy.[27] Luther offered another set of theses for what has
become known as the Heidelberg Disputation, in which he
explained and defended his new understanding of the
gospel—which Brecht believes may have come to him
only shortly before this meeting—and also showed himself
to have become a penetratingly original theologian.

In the Heidelberg Disputation, he made his famous distinction between the "theology of glory" and the "theology of the cross." God chose to reveal Himself, not in His
glory, but in a lowly manger and in suffering and dying on

the cross. Some people look for God in terms of glory—expecting clear answers and perfect understanding, wanting all their problems solved, looking for faith to give them a life of success. They put their emphasis on works and achievements, strength and power. And yet God makes Himself known instead in weakness, failure, and suffering. When we bear our own cross, we are forced to depend not on ourselves but on Jesus, who meets us in our suffering, which He took into Himself on His cross.

Thus began one of Luther's most impressive achievements: developing a theology of suffering that was both realistic and comforting. In his theology of the cross he also developed a kind of spirituality that avoided the dangers of mysticism in favor of an approach to the spiritual life that was both Christ-centered and grounded in human reality.[28]

Luther also had his chance to debate the theology of the medieval church—the purpose of his original theses on indulgences—when a disputation was arranged at the University of Leipzig. Luther's former (and future) enemy Karlstadt had joined the fray with an attack on the formidable Vatican theologian John Eck. Theses and counter-theses were exchanged. Eck challenged Karlstadt to a public debate. Leipzig agreed to be the host. Since the issues had to do with Luther, he was invited to take part.

On June 24, 1519, two hundred armed Wittenberg students escorted Luther and Karlstadt, along with other faculty members and a wagon load of books, to Leipzig. As the procession entered the city, Karlstadt's wagon tipped over due to a broken wheel, and he was injured. He still took his turns debating Eck, though Luther was the main show. The debate, attended by people from far and wide, lasted seventeen days.

Though they debated indulgences and the assurance of salvation and justification by faith, the issue kept coming down to the competing authorities of the pope versus the Bible. Luther, perhaps falling into Eck's trap, publicly denied the supremacy of the pope, saying that the papacy was merely a human invention whose claims to supreme authority were only four hundred years old.

The humanist scholar Petrus Mosellanus, who attended the Leipzig Disputation, has given us a vivid description of Luther. Notice that while most of our portraits of Luther are from his later life, showing him to be a big, hulking man, at the time of the indulgences controversy, Luther was a monk in his thirties, thin and gaunt, no doubt from a combination of monastic self-denial and his recurring health problems. But Mosellanus nails not only Luther's appearance but his personality:

> Martin is of medium height with a gaunt body that has been so exhausted by studies and worries that one can almost count the bones under his skin; yet he is manly and vigorous, with a high, clear voice. He is full of learning and has an excellent knowledge of the Scriptures, so that he can refer to facts as if they were at his fingers' tips. He knows enough Greek and Hebrew to enable him to pass judgments on interpretations. He is also not lacking in subject material and has a large store of words and ideas. In his life and behavior he is very courteous and friendly, and there is nothing of the stern stoic or grumpy fellow about him. He can adjust to all occasions.

In a social gather he is gay, witty, lively, ever full of joy, always has a bright and happy face, no matter how seriously his adversaries threaten him. One can see in him that God's strength is with him in his difficult undertaking. The only fault everyone criticizes in him is that he is somewhat too violent and cutting in his reprimands, in fact more than is proper for one seeking to find new trails in theology, and certainly also for a divine; this is probably a weakness of all those who have gained their learning somewhat late.[29]

This combination of a good-natured, humorous, and likable personality with a polemical harshness against his opponents characterizes Luther and his writings for the rest of his days.

Luther was also an indefatigable preacher, and his sermons were printed and widely distributed among the common people. He did not write only about the controversial issues. At this time he wrote treatises designed to teach ordinary people the truths of Christianity (works on the Ten Commandments and the Apostles' Creed), to show them how to pray (a commentary on the Lord's Prayer), and devotional works of spiritual comfort (on suffering, on how to prepare to die). He also wrote about issues of everyday life, about marriage and parenthood and how these too are holy callings from God, about economic abuses and good government—everything connected to the gospel and to the life of faith. When he wrote about the sacraments, he showed that baptism and the Lord's Supper are both all about *justification,* the work of Christ to be received by faith. Good works, in turn, are not religious rituals but the fruit of faith as it is lived out in ordinary life.

Two works in particular need to be mentioned here, both written in the tumultuous but remarkably productive year of 1520. *The Babylonian Captivity of the Church* examined the sacramental system of the Church of Rome, trimming down the number of biblically warranted sacraments from seven to two (baptism and the Lord's Supper) and reinterpreting those according to the gospel. He also indicated with his title that the church had been in a state of captivity like ancient Israel and that now it could be free again. This work significantly raised the stakes. The controversy was no longer simply over indulgences, whose abuses were recognized by many good Catholics, but over the institutional makeup and the practices of the church itself. This in-your-face challenge could not be ignored by Rome.

One of Luther's greatest works is *The Freedom of the Christian.* It opens with a friendly letter to Pope Leo X, to whom the book is dedicated, urging the pope not to listen to his advisers who try to exalt him over Scripture and over God himself, but to embrace the role of servant of Christ, not Christ's substitute. Luther then offers him this treatise on the Christian life, which develops the paradox:

> A Christian is a perfectly free lord of all, subject to none.
> A Christian is a perfectly dutiful servant of all, subject to all.[30]

The gospel brings *freedom*—from the bondage of sin, the burden of the law, the fear of damnation, the petty constraints of legalism. Luther daringly developed here a notion that would later blossom into what we now know as political freedom, his doctrine of the priesthood of all believers, that all callings and all Christians share an equal status before God:

> Faith is produced and preserved in us by preaching why Christ came, what he brought and bestowed, what benefit it is to us to accept him. This is done when that Christian liberty which he bestows is rightly taught and we are told in what way we Christians are all kings and priests and therefore lords of all and may firmly believe that whatever we have done is pleasing and acceptable in the sight of God.[31]

But this faith and this freedom are to be lived out in love and service to our neighbor. The Christian freely denies himself in order to serve others. Faith bears fruit in "the love which makes us free, joyful, almighty workers and conquerors over all tribulations, servants of our neighbors, yet lords of all."[32] In one of Luther's memorable expressions, "Each one should become as it were a Christ to the other that we may be Christs to one another and Christ may be the same in all, that is, that we may be truly Christians."[33]

By the time the pope's bull was published and the order went out to throw Luther's works into the fire, there was already a lot to burn.

BEFORE THE EMPEROR

*T*HE DIET OF WORMS (pronounced "vormz") was the nineteen-year-old emperor's first such assembly with the princes of his realm. The princes who were bishops, along with the pope's representatives, wanted Charles to arrest Luther immediately. Elector Frederick persuaded him not to act on the ban before giving Luther a hearing.

Charles himself had been critical of the pope, who had conspired against his election. (The pope did not want the Hapsburg family to create a powerful dynasty, with Maximilian's grandson getting the empire, which is exactly what happened.) If Charles was not particularly sympathetic to the pope, neither were most of the princes, who regularly complained about the financial abuses of the church. The princes also expressed the fear that Luther had become so popular, if he were condemned without a trial, the common people would rise up in riots and rebellion.

Nevertheless, Charles was very pious, and he considered part of his duties as emperor to protect Christianity and to oppose heresy. It was one thing to oppose the pope in his political machinations, but hardly anyone questioned his authority in the church, and everyone feared the spiritual penalties he could impose.

A compromise, of sorts, was arranged. Charles issued a mandate to his realms to enforce the ban. But first Luther would be summoned to the diet under a promise of safe conduct. He would not be permitted to debate his position. He would be asked if he confessed the beliefs expressed in his writings that had been defined as heretical. He would be given the opportunity to recant them. If he did, then the diet would hear him on other matters, such as the abuses in the church. If he would not recant, the princes would agree to act against him, though they requested that the diet take up the issue of the complaints against Rome.

Luther was summoned on March 6, 1521. He said that he would go to Worms to be executed, if need be, but not to recant.

He left Wittenberg on April 2. The city gave him a covered wagon for the ride, and the university gave him twenty gulden for his expenses. He was joined by four or five fellow monks. On the journey, they passed the time by Luther expounding the book of Joshua as an image of the gospel. The cities they passed through along the way received Luther as a hero, welcoming him with crowds and banquets in his honor. Luther would say later that it made him think of Christ's triumphal entry, but also of what happened to Christ after that.

After a journey of two weeks, he arrived in Worms. The emperor's herald (a sympathizer) led him in and announced him with trumpets as two thousand towns-people filled the streets.

The next day, April 17, at 4:00 p.m., he was brought before the diet, which was meeting at the bishop's residence next to the cathedral. Luther came in laughing, looking around the hall and speaking to a friend he saw in the crowd. Acting this way in the emperor's presence was considered a serious breach of etiquette, which Luther, unfamiliar with courtly protocol, did not realize. He was told to be quiet and not to speak unless told to.

The emperor's spokesman was Johann von der Eck, a church official. (This was *not* the same John Eck that Luther debated in print and at Leipzig, despite the similarity of their names.) He spoke to Luther first in Latin and then in German. Von der Eck told him that he had been summoned before the emperor and the diet for two reasons. First, to determine if certain books published under his name were his. Second, to determine if Luther still confessed the beliefs expressed in those books or if he wished to recant them.

Luther's books were piled on a table in front of him. He was asked if he had written these books. Before he could answer, his legal adviser, provided by Elector Frederick, called for the titles to be read. They were.

Luther replied first in German then in Latin. He spoke quietly, nervously, and was hard to understand. He said that the books were his. In fact, he had written more.

Did he stand by what he said in those books or did he recant?

Luther replied that the matter concerned faith, salvation, and the Word of God. It would be presumptuous, he said, to answer in haste, lest he risk denying Christ. He asked for time to think.

Von der Eck told him not to topple Christianity by his private opinions. If he recanted, the emperor would intercede for him with the pope. But if he still affirmed these opinions, the emperor would protect the church. The archbishop admonished him that he should have known why he had been brought here, but the emperor would give him one day to consider his answer.

The next day, the diet met in a bigger hall to accommodate the crowds. The conference was behind schedule and did not get to Luther until 6:00 p.m. The hall was lit by torches.

Von der Eck repeated the questions. Luther answered first in German and then in Latin, but this time in a loud, clear voice that everyone could hear. He began by apologizing for his ignorance of courtly manners and said that his books were of three kinds. Some were teachings about piety and morals, which even his opponents recognized as being useful and appropriate for Christians to read. He should not recant those. Another group was about abuses of the papacy that were destroying Christianity and harming the German nation. He could not recant those either. The last group of books were those written against individual people who defended the tyranny of Rome or questioned the piety he was advocating. Luther admitted that he had written too harshly, but he could not take back those books because to do so would confirm tyranny and godlessness. He said, however, that if anything he had written could be shown to be an error by the testimony of Scripture, he would recant it and be the first to burn his books. As for his threatening the unity of the church, there would always be conflicts when people defy the Word of God.

It was sweltering hot in the hall, and Luther was perspiring heavily. The elector's lawyer proposed that Luther not be required to reply in Latin. Luther refused the offer and repeated the whole discourse in the other language.

Von der Eck said that the emperor was to be praised for his patience in listening to such a long speech, even though what was said about the pope was inappropriate. He disagreed about the distinction between the three types of books. Luther was acting like other heretics in advancing his personal opinions over the testimony of the universal church. Did he believe he was the only one who understood the Scriptures? Did he presume to exalt his interpretation over that of so many of the church's holy scholars and noted theologians over the centuries? Von der Eck demanded that Luther give a simple answer: Do you or do you not recant your books and the errors they contain?

Whereupon Luther gave his famous answer:

> Unless I am convinced by the testimony of the Scriptures or by clear reason (for I do not trust either in the pope or in councils alone, since it is well known that they have often erred and contradicted themselves), I am bound by the Scriptures I have quoted and my conscience is captive to the Word of God. I cannot and I will not retract anything, since it is neither safe nor right to go against conscience. I cannot do otherwise, here I stand, may God help me, amen.[34]

Pandemonium broke out. The emperor rose to his feet, saying he had had enough. The meeting broke up. Two of the emperor's men escorted Luther out of the hall as a Spanish attendant cried out, "Into the fire with him!" As he left the building, Luther raised his fist in the gesture of a knight victorious at a tournament. Some say he said, "I have come through, I have come through!" Others report that he said, "I am finished!"[35]

He had stood alone against the powers of his world. Because he had a place to stand.

THE KNIGHT IN
THE CASTLE

*T*HE NEXT DAY THE emperor made a speech to the diet saying that he would have to defend Christianity and suppress Luther as a heretic. The princes asked that a commission of scholars meet with Luther to give him one last chance. The emperor agreed, granting three more days for Luther to recant. The discussions were surprisingly positive, but they were to no avail. On April 25 Luther learned that the emperor would act against him but that his safe-conduct pass would still be honored. He had twenty-one days to return to Wittenberg, where, presumably, Frederick would have to arrest him.

The emperor drew up the Edict of Worms to ban Luther and his teachings and to require his arrest. In the meantime, wars were breaking out and many of the princes had other obligations, so the members of the diet were dispersing. Only a small number were present to approve the edict.

The Edict of Worms declared Luther a heretic. No one was to give him food or shelter. Whoever found him was to take him prisoner and bring him to the emperor. The same applied to Luther's supporters. Anyone could seize their property. Reading and distributing Luther's writings was outlawed.

Elector Frederick went to the emperor, asking that he be exempt from having to serve Luther with the edict. Strangely, the young emperor could not say no to the man who had helped put him into office, and he agreed with the request.

In the meantime, Luther and his party headed home to Wittenberg. They traveled in a covered wagon and toward evening were going through a forest. Suddenly they were attacked by horsemen with crossbows. Luther's companions fled as the assailants aimed their crossbows at the driver and forced him to identify his passenger. They pulled Luther from the back. He grabbed his New Testament and his Hebrew Bible and rode away with his captors.

Shortly before midnight the kidnappers brought him to a remote castle known as the Wartburg. They turned out not to be bandits, nor zealots enforcing the Edict of Worms. They were Elector Frederick's men, and they were saving Luther's life.

From the point of view of the rest of the empire and the Church of Rome, Luther had simply disappeared. Many of his followers assumed he had been killed, that the emperor had violated his safe-conduct agreement.

At the castle Luther was told to exchange his monk's habit for the garb of a knight. He was to grow out his tonsure—the shaved top of his head that was the mark of a monk—and to grow a beard. He was to go by the name of Knight George. He was given two boys of noble birth to serve as his pages. He was given two adjoining rooms and everything he needed.

Luther at first was miserable in the Wartburg. He felt like a hermit. He was lonely. He had spells of sickness. The old spiritual torments came back. He felt that demons were attacking him. (He is said to have thrown an inkwell at one.) He did not, however, question his convictions.

Once, to alleviate his boredom, his wardens took him hunting. He did not like it. He felt sorry for the animals. At one point, he tried to save a little rabbit by catching it and hiding it in the sleeve of his cloak. The dogs, though, sniffed it out, jumped up, and bit through Luther's clothes, killing the rabbit. Luther interpreted it as a parable for how the devil, with his dogs, the godless bishops and theologians, pursued souls, killing the ones that Luther was trying to save.

But at the Wartburg, with its forced isolation that kept Luther from his busy routine of lecturing, preaching, writing theology, and engaging in polemics, Luther did his most important work of all. He translated the Bible.

To that point, the Bible was known only in a Latin translation, the so-called Vulgate, the work of Saint Jerome in the fourth century. The Bible in its original languages, Hebrew and Greek, was all but unknown, as those languages were forgotten in Western Europe after the fall of Rome.

The Renaissance, though, came about largely through the rediscovery of Greek, one of the better legacies of the

Crusades. When scholars learned to read Greek, this gave Europe access to the great works of classical civilization, which inspired a "new birth" of education, the arts, and the humanities.

The rediscovery of Greek also meant access to the New Testament in its original language. Erasmus, the greatest of the Renaissance humanists, studied the manuscripts of the Greek New Testament, and in a remarkable scholarly achievement, in 1516 published an edition of the Greek New Testament.

Luther, a Renaissance scholar himself, knew Greek—and Hebrew—and studied the Bible in its original languages. For ordinary Christians, though, who did not even know Latin, let alone Greek and Hebrew, the Bible was a closed book.

Luther believed that God worked through His Word. He was convinced that the Bible was not just historical information, though it was that, but that the Holy Spirit worked in and through the Word of God, convicting people of sin and bringing them to Christ. The only way to change the church—and the lives of its members—was not through power, not through the sword, but through the Word.

Luther wanted every Christian to have access to the Word of God. So he took upon himself the task of translating the Bible into German, the language of his people.

This was the first vernacular translation that was not derived from the Latin version, the first since Jerome to be based on the original languages. Luther's translation was a monumental act of scholarship. But it was also a monumental literary achievement.

We have already seen Luther's mastery of language in his incisive explanations of theological truths and in the personal expressiveness of his style. As a preacher accustomed to proclaiming the Word of God orally, he had mastered the art of connecting with ordinary people and communicating to them effectively. He said that he tried to listen to the speech of mothers in the home, children in the street, men and women in the marketplace, and the butcher and the tradesmen in their shops. He "looked them on the mouth," he said, and tried to craft a language for them.[36] In addition, Luther was gifted as a poet and a musician, as we shall see when he began to write great hymns.

In bringing these literary gifts to his translation of the Bible, Luther managed to render the Word of God in such a way that it was not only clear but eloquent. To this day his translation is heralded for its accuracy, power, and beauty. Its language is both down to earth and rich and evocative.

As a preacher, Luther was sensitive to the sound and cadence of language. His translation of the Bible would soar when read from the pulpit. Musicians, such as Bach, would find it perfectly suited to be put to music.

With his translation of the Bible, Luther became, in effect, the father of modern German. Before Luther's Bible, there was no single German tongue; each separate principality spoke a different dialect that in many cases was all but indecipherable to the others. Luther's Bible became so widely accepted, so thoroughly read, internalized, and emulated that it created a standard German language.[37]

Luther's Bible is still the standard German Bible in use today. It became the model, in its style and in many of its expressions, for the other vernacular Bibles that would come later, including particularly the King James Version in English. That translation was the work of a committee of fifty-four scholars. Luther did his translation virtually by himself.

Translating the entire New Testament took him less than eleven weeks.

In March he started revising his first draft and preparing the manuscript for publication. He enlisted the aid of Philip Melanchthon, perhaps his closest friend, who would prove to be another key figure in Luther's reforms.

Melanchthon is considered to be second only to Erasmus in the ranks of the great Renaissance classicists. A master of classical languages, his books on rhetoric and education became staples of the Renaissance curriculum. He was a humanities professor at Wittenberg who embraced the gospel that Luther was preaching.

Though a layman, Melanchthon joined in Luther's theological work. And Luther considered him a better Bible commentator than he was. The two became close friends and co-workers.

When Luther was in the Wartburg, only a few knew of his whereabouts. Among them were Melanchthon and Spalatin, with whom Luther kept in touch with extensive letter writing. It was Melanchthon who urged Luther to translate the New Testament so that the people could see for themselves what the epistles of Paul had to say. He and Spalatin sent Luther the dictionaries, reference books, and commentaries he would need.

Later Luther asked Melanchthon to review the manuscript and check his Greek. The result was a number of helpful changes and suggestions. The New Testament, illustrated by woodcuts by his friend the Wittenberg artist Lucas Cranach, was published in September 1522.

The Old Testament took much longer. Melanchthon, with his expertise in Hebrew, played a bigger role in helping Luther with that project. By this time Luther was back in Wittenberg, busy with enormous tasks, as we shall see. He no longer had the enforced leisure that he had in the Wartburg, which allowed him to devote all of his time to the New Testament. He decided to publish the Old Testament in parts, as he completed them. The first was published in mid-1523. The second was sent to the printer on December 4, 1523, and was available to the public early that next year. The third part bogged him down. Luther said that the language of the book of Job was so difficult that it would sometimes take him four days to translate three lines. He published the poetic books in the fall of 1524. However, the prophets—completing the Bible—did not appear until 1532.

When the Bible was available in the language of the people, it sold out immediately and went through printing after printing. It was not long before one of Luther's Romanist enemies, Johann Cochlaeus, was complaining:

> Luther's New Testament was so much multiplied and
> spread by printers that even tailors and shoemakers, yea,
> even women and ignorant persons who had accepted
> this new Lutheran gospel, and could read a little German, studied it with the greatest avidity as the fountain

of all truth. Some committed it to memory, and carried it about in their bosom. In a few months such people deemed themselves so learned that they were not ashamed to dispute about faith and the gospel not only with Catholic laymen, but even with priests and monks and doctors of divinity.[38]

Luther's Bible was a runaway best seller, enriching lots of printers, but he refused to take any money for the Bible or for any of his writings. His New Testament translation sold for a half gulden for unbound pages or one or one and a half gulden, depending on the binding. About the price of an indulgence.

CHAOS

*T*HE EDICT OF WORMS had an unintended conse-
quence. In casting not only Luther but everyone who agreed with him out of the Roman Catholic
Church, the edict shattered Christendom. Those thrown
out of the Roman Catholic Church now had to start
churches of their own.

Up to this point, Luther's goal was to reform the church,
but the church repudiated him and what he was trying to
do. It is often said that Luther split from the Roman
Catholic Church. That is not true. He was thrown out of
the Roman Catholic Church. There is a huge difference.
Luther was no schismatic. He did not start some new religion on his own authority. He did not dream up some new
theology. He was trying to bring the church back to its true
nature and its true message, as defined by the Word of
God, which the church itself professed to believe.

The Roman Church, in turn, refused to take the concerns seriously, much less give them a genuine hearing.
The pope refused to address even the most flagrant abuses
that were obvious to everyone. Instead of listening to

those who questioned its direction, the Roman Church tried to destroy them. Thus the Roman Catholic Church created Protestantism.

For the ordinary people who had embraced the evangelical faith—which was what Luther's theology was called, from "evangel," meaning gospel—the realization that they were no long under the yoke of Rome was exhilarating. No more oppressive church taxes and fees. No more canon laws regulating what they had to do. More than that, no crushing guilt. No fear of purgatory. The assurance of salvation. As they read Luther, they began to realize the freedom of a Christian.

But they were also biblically illiterate. Most of them were totally illiterate. They had so much energy that had been pent up for so long. When the structures that held them down were removed, they exploded.

Throughout Saxony riots broke out. In Erfurt a mob of twelve hundred students, workers, and ne'er-do-wells demolished the homes of sixty Catholic priests, who barely escaped with their lives.[39] In Wittenberg a group of students, armed with knives, interrupted the mass at the City Church, chasing out the priests.

In response to Luther's criticism of churchly vows, monks were leaving the monasteries and priests were marrying, which Luther approved of, but many of them could not support themselves. There was a spirit of disorder, with no one knowing what to do.

Luther had wanted Melanchthon to direct the reformation of the church at Wittenberg, but since Melanchthon was a layman, the city council placed Andreas Karlstadt in charge of the church.

Though Karlstadt had once criticized Luther in his first years at Wittenberg for being insufficiently Catholic, now he went to the other extreme. Karlstadt not only abolished the mass, he abolished all orders of worship. He no longer wore vestments but just preached. The laity were given both elements in Holy Communion (that is, both the bread and the wine; only priests had received the wine previously), which was in line with Luther's teachings. But then Karlstadt started teaching that not taking both elements was a sin. He married then said that for a priest *not* to be married was a sin. Having been freed from the legalism of Catholicism, Karlstadt imposed a legalism of his own.

Then Karlstadt questioned the value of baptism. Then he questioned the value of the Lord's Supper. Then he questioned the value of the Bible.

As a scholar he had published a treatise that in many ways anticipated the higher critical method of today's theological liberals, questioning whether Moses wrote the Pentateuch and saying that some of the books of the Bible lacked historic evidence.[40] But then he came under the influence of some self-styled "prophets" from Zwickau who taught that the Holy Spirit inspired believers directly. With these personal revelations, there was no need for the Bible.

Karlstadt turned against his own profession and his own field of theology, teaching that learning is not necessary since the Holy Spirit will reveal all we need to know. He told the students to leave the university and take up agriculture. He closed the city's boys' school and turned it into a bakery. He started dressing like a peasant and taught that all human titles were sinful.[41]

It was not just Karlstadt. The Wittenberg city council passed a new church constitution requiring that all altars, images, and crosses would be removed from the sanctuaries and burned; the endowments that funded the churches would be broken up and distributed to the poor; and everyone was allowed to preach.

Before the council could act, mobs rushed into the churches, smashing images and vandalizing the property.

Elector Frederick finally stepped in. He had been remarkably patient in letting the church take its new form. But the religious turmoil had turned into social disorder. He canceled the constitution, allowed for some reforms in the mass but insisted on church order, and forbade Karlstadt from preaching, replacing him with Nicholas von Amsdorf, an ally of Luther's.

But the church still needed leadership. Melanchthon tried to hold things together, but he was an intellectual, not a leader. Karlstadt and the "prophets" ran roughshod over him.

Melanchthon and other Christians wrote Luther, begging him to come back. When Luther heard what was happening, he knew he had to return.

The elector warned him not to, that if he did, he might have to send him to the emperor. Luther wrote back, saying that he was protected by God, so he would protect the elector rather than the elector protecting him. If the emperor demanded that the elector hand him over, he should do so and not rebel. Luther wanted to stop the rebellion.

On March 5, 1522, at great risk to his life, traveling through the lands of Catholic enemies sworn to kill him, he came back to Wittenberg. He assumed the office of preacher at the city church. Luther believed that only the Word of God could quell the disorder and create true evangelical reform. He would put down the chaos not by the use of the force but by preaching.

Upon his return, he preached every day for a week. The churches were packed. You know that you have been freed from God's wrath, he admonished them, but something is wrong. You lack love, the fruit of faith. Love puts the needs of the weaker brethren ahead of one's own. Love never uses force. You need the Word of God, which will change your heart, create right worship, and eliminate idolatry.

Here is a sample from his second sermon:

> I will preach, speak, write, but I will force no one; for faith must be voluntary. Take me as an example. I stood up against the Pope, indulgences, and all papists, but without violence or uproar. I only urged, preached, and declared God's Word, nothing else. And yet while I was asleep, or drinking Wittenberg beer with Philip Melanchthon and Amsdorf, the Word inflicted greater injury on popery than prince or emperor ever did. I did nothing, the Word did everything. Had I appealed to force, all Germany might have been deluged with blood; yea, I might have kindled a conflict at Worms, so that the Emperor would not have been safe. But what would have been the result? Ruin and desolation of body and soul. I therefore kept quiet, and gave the Word free course through the world. Do you know what the Devil thinks when he sees men use violence to propagate the gospel? He sits with

folded arms behind the fire of hell, and says with malignant looks and frightful grin: "Ah, how wise these madmen are to play my game! Let them go on; I shall reap the benefit. I delight in it." But when he sees the Word running and contending alone on the battle-field, then he shudders and shakes for fear. The Word is almighty, and takes captive the hearts.[42]

Luther could thunder, but these sermons were surprisingly gentle. They had a remarkable effect. The people were chastened. Even many of the radicals and leaders of the violence repented. Not Karlstadt, who retired to the country to live his self-chosen peasant life, and not the Zwickau prophets, who were driven out of town. But the church and the community came together while Luther planned an orderly, peaceful reformation.

REFORMS

*I*N THE MONTHS AND years that followed, Luther reformed the mass by removing the invocations to
the saints, the language that called the Lord's Supper a
sacrifice, and other elements that went against the gospel.
Other elements, though—the confession of sins, the
prayers, the readings from Scripture, the sermon, the celebration of Holy Communion, all punctuated by ancient
songs of supplication and praise—were retained. Their
very language came from the Bible. They conveyed the
gospel. In fact, Luther said that the gospel was preserved
throughout the darkness of the papal abuses in the liturgy
of the church. Every time the *Agnus Dei* was sung—"O,
Christ, thou Lamb of God, who taketh away the sins of
the world, have mercy on us"—the gospel was being proclaimed, and God's Word was never without effect in
bringing people to Himself.

The worship service thus followed the historic liturgy,
but though Latin continued to be used where it was understood, the liturgy itself was put in the language of the peo-

ple. The sermon, which had dwindled to a cursory moralistic homily during the Middle Ages, became central, focusing on the proclamation of the gospel and the application of Scripture. The worship service was also punctuated by hymns, many of which, as will be discussed later, were written by Luther.

Church art that pointed away from Christ and the gospel was removed. That included images of saints, icons of the Virgin Mary, and the like. Art that pointed to Christ and expressed the gospel and the Word of God was retained. That included crucifixes, crosses, pictures drawn from the Bible, and Christian symbolism. Visual images were not to be venerated in the medieval fashion, but Luther denied that they were intrinsically idolatrous. Someone with faith in Christ does not worship a false god, and the use of art—as in the woodcuts illustrating his Bible—is within Christian freedom and can be useful for teaching and meditation.[43]

Luther also promoted education. Now that Bibles were available in German, people needed to be taught to read them. Melanchthon devised a challenging curriculum, applying principles of Renaissance classical education to the instruction of young children. Students not only learned to read, they learned to develop all of their intellectual gifts. Luther insisted that girls too should go to school, something that rarely happened even in wealthy families. The peasants too should have access to the Bible and thus to education, concepts that would prove revolutionary.

Luther urged cities, nobles, and churches to open schools, and they did. The university was also reformed, with the old scholastic, Aristotelian curriculum replaced with Renaissance-style humanities and the Bible taking the central place in the study of theology.

As he was writing, consulting, solving disputes, and meeting with people, above all Luther was exercising his leadership by preaching. Wittenberg had a congregation of two thousand people who met in two different church buildings. Luther was assigned to preach, but the pastoral duties were held by John Bugenhagen, a capable evangelical pastor who worked well with Luther and shared the preaching load. Two deacons—the equivalent of assistant pastors—also helped with preaching and the pastoral care of the members. When Bugenhagen was away spreading the Reformation to other regions, as he often was, Luther took over his pastoral duties—hearing confessions (a practice that Luther retained), counseling those with problems, and conducting baptisms and presiding at the Lord's Supper.

Luther came to realize that while all believers were priests, not everyone was called to be a pastor. Those who led churches needed to be well educated in the Scriptures. Luther argued that congregations should have the right to choose their own pastors rather than have them appointed by bishops or by secular rulers.

Church services at Wittenberg were intense. There were two services every day, one in the morning and one in the afternoon. On Mondays and Tuesdays the sermons in these services focused on the catechism; that is, the basic texts of the Ten Commandments, the Lord's Prayer, and the Apostles' Creed. Wednesdays featured sermons on the gospel of Matthew. Thursdays and Fridays the sermons focused on the epistles. Saturdays concentrated on the gospel of John.

There were three services on Sundays: matins at 6:00 a.m., with a sermon on an epistle reading for the day; mass at 8:00 or 9:00 a.m., with a sermon on the gospel reading; and vespers in the afternoon, with a sermon on an Old Testament text.

One year Luther preached 121 times. On forty of those days he preached twice a day.

Frederick the Wise died in 1525, before the reforms were fully implemented. He was succeeded as elector by his brother, John the Steadfast, who was a zealous follower of the evangelical cause.

Other prominent princes—the rulers of Brandenburg, Hesse, Anhalt, Lüneberg, Würtenberg, Pomerania, Nassau, Brunswick-Calenburg—also joined Luther's movement. Duke George of Albertine Saxony was Luther's most fire-breathing enemy, but when he died, the new duke embraced his gospel. Cities throughout the empire—including the free imperial cities with their semi-autonomous governments—proved to be particularly fertile ground for the Reformation.[44]

Luther's Reformation spread out of Germany. The king of Denmark became an evangelical. With the help of Bugenhagen and other evangelical preachers Luther brought in, he reformed the churches not only in Denmark but in Norway and Iceland, which were under his influence. Then the king of Sweden embraced Lutheranism, as did his territory Finland.[45]

The former Hussites in Bohemia, present-day Czechoslovakia, viewed Luther's work as the continuing legacy of the martyred Jan Hus, so they joined the Reformation. Also attracted to the Lutheran reformation were principalities in Poland and Hungary and as far away as Latvia.[46]

In England, Henry VIII wrote a blistering attack on Luther, which earned for the British crown the title "Defender of the Faith" from the pope, a title that English monarchs still hold. Luther fired back with a little book called *Against Henry, King of England* (1522), with a harshness and lack of deference that kings were not accustomed to hearing. That was somewhat shocking at the time. But then in 1534 Henry staged a reformation of his own, breaking from the Roman Church so that he could divorce Catherine of Aragon and marry Anne Boleyn. This brought in Lutherans to help shape the new church, and Thomas Cramner's *Book of Common Prayer* was greatly influenced by the Lutheran liturgy.

But as the Reformation spread, so did persecution. The first to die, due to the Edict of Worms, were two young Dutch Augustinians, John van den Esschen and Henry Vos, who were burned at the stake in Brussels. When Luther heard the news, he cried. He said, "I thought I would be the first to be martyred for the sake of this holy gospel; but I am not worthy of it."[47]

The martyrdom of the two young men—for following his teachings—moved Luther greatly. It inspired him to write a song about them, his first attempt at poetry and music writing, bringing out an artistic gift that would result in some of the greatest hymns of all time.

The song was a ballad that would go by the name "A Lovely Hymn About the Two Martyrs of Christ Who Were Burned in Brussels by the Sophists of Louvain." The last stanza uses natural imagery of the coming of spring to describe the hand of God in the new work He had started:

> Even at the door is summer nigh,
> The winter now is ended,
> The tender flowers come out and spy;
> His hand whence once extended
> Withdraws not till he's finished.[48]

THE SPLIT WITH HUMANISM

*W*HILE LUTHER WAS DEALING with intensifying opposition from Rome, even as his reforms were going forward, he soon found himself clashing with many people who had formerly been his allies.

At first, the Reformation and the Renaissance went hand in hand, mutually supporting each other. The humanists' recovery of the Greek language, their critique of scholasticism, and their emphasis on original sources helped to pave the way for the Reformers. The University of Wittenberg was a Renaissance institution. Melanchthon was one of the movement's major figures. Erasmus edited the Greek New Testament that made possible Luther's translation.

The word *humanism* originally referred to the "humanities," that is, the new learning that emphasized literature, languages, and the classics. And yet the newer sense of the term—faith in the power and greatness of human beings—arguably had its beginnings with the Renaissance humanists.

Though Erasmus agreed with Luther's attacks on the abuses in the church and in the early days supported his attack on indulgences, he became troubled with Luther's high view of sin and his low view of human nature. In 1524 Erasmus published *A Diatribe or Discourse Concerning Free Choice* in which he specifically targeted Luther's teaching that we cannot by our own powers choose to be good or to follow God.

Luther replied by writing one of his greatest theological treatises, *The Bondage of the Will* (1525). With his customary vehemence and biting wit, Luther took on one of the greatest minds of his day, defining the essential differences between a world view that is humanistic and one that is biblical.

Luther argued that the human will is in bondage. That is, as the New Testament puts it, we are slaves to sin. The Fall is such that human nature is radically corrupted and limited. Yes, we have a free will in matters that are "below us," that is, we can freely choose what food to eat or what path to walk. But we cannot choose what is "above us," namely, in spiritual matters. We have to depend utterly on the grace of God, who gives us the gift of faith and changes our heart through His Word and the work of Christ. Then and only then are Christians free from the power of sin. Christ frees us, whereupon we are free indeed.

But Luther's difference with Erasmus went further than this. Luther showed Erasmus to be basically a moralist who reduced the Christian faith to a list of easily followed virtues; he was a rationalist who blithely thought he could reason God into submission with little need for

God's self-revelation in His Word. In short, Erasmus was essentially the same as the Roman Catholics, who likewise believed that people could will themselves into salvation, save themselves by their freely chosen works, and rationalize away the Scriptures with their systematic theologies constructed by human reason. And, indeed, Erasmus never left Roman Catholicism, nor did he ever pose enough of a threat to attract the pope's wrath. (One could argue that the popes of that day were, in fact, Renaissance humanists, what with their Sistine Chapels and their human-centered preoccupations.)

After this controversy between Luther and Erasmus, the Reformation and the Renaissance, once in harmony, began to go in different directions. Renaissance humanism, once Christian, would develop into the Enlightenment, into materialism, into secular humanism, and all of the human-centered philosophies of the modern and postmodern world.

KATE, MY RIB

*I*N MARCH 1523 LUTHER received a letter that had
been smuggled to him by Leonhard Koppe, a
merchant. It was addressed to the "highly learned Dr.
Martinus Luther at Wittenberg" and it was from a group
of eleven nuns at the convent of Marienthron. The
spokeswoman for the group said they had read Luther's
writings and had become convinced that life in the cloister was not necessary for their soul's salvation and that it
had become intolerable. They wanted to leave, and they
were willing to take the consequences. They said they
had appealed to their relatives, but they were unwilling to
help. They knew of no one else to turn to other than the
person who had changed their thinking by Christ's gospel
and his own courage.[49]

Luther thought about the matter for some time, then
he wrote back, agreeing that it was a wrong practice to
force very young girls into a convent and to keep them
there against their will. He also acknowledged that they

were being prevented from hearing the Word of God. He agreed to do what he could to help them escape.

He turned the problem over to Koppe, who had a good idea. He had a regular business with the convent, selling supplies and delivering them in his wagon. On the evening of April 6 Koppe took his wagon into the convent. It was loaded with herring barrels. When he drove out, eleven of the barrels contained nuns. The next morning, which was Easter, they climbed out of their barrels and were free.

One of the eleven was twenty-four-year-old Katharina von Bora. Her parents were minor nobility who had sent her into the convent when she had turned six years old. This was not uncommon at the time. That was a good way to get rid of a daughter. Her father had a title, but big money problems, and this way he would not have to come up with a large dowry with which to marry her off. Besides, giving a daughter to the Lord would count as a "good work" to help him get into heaven.

Now Luther had the problem of trying to figure out what to do with the young women. They had no money; their families, despite pleas from Luther, wanted nothing to do with them. Luther helped to arrange marriages for some of them. Others found work as maids.

Katharina was taken into the household of Lucas Cranach, the court painter who became the great artist of the Reformation. To him we owe most of the portraits of its key players so that we know what they looked like. Cranach was quite an entrepreneur, setting up, among other things, a publishing business. Thus Cranach not only illustrated Luther's Bible with his woodcuts, he printed it on his printing press and sold it. Cranach was on the city council of Wittenberg and at one point served as mayor, giving Luther what would become crucial support from the city. Katharina was more than a maid in the Cranach household. She apparently became something like the manager of the household, and the Cranachs treated her like a daughter.

Katharina was courted by a young man, Jerome Baumgartner, from a wealthy Nuremberg family, but the relationship was suddenly broken off, likely because his parents disapproved of his marrying someone without a dowry.

In those days of arranged marriages, Luther tried to help, setting her up with Dr. Kaspar Glatz, a Wittenberg professor and pastor of a nearby church. His nickname was "Glacius," that is, "Icy." Katharina did not like him. She complained to Nicholas von Amsdorf, Luther's friend and co-worker. "What's wrong with him?" the theology professor naive in the ways of the heart asked her. "Isn't someone who is a doctor, a professor, a pastor, good enough for you?" She reportedly replied that she would be willing to have a doctor, a professor, and a pastor, but not Icy Glatz. She told Amsdorf that she would be willing to marry either him or Luther.

When Luther heard that, he was taken aback. He had never seriously thought of marriage for himself. He had been writing about marriage as a high calling from God, superior to the false vows of celibacy required by the papacy, and he had encouraged other monks and pastors to marry. He had said earlier that he would not take on a family for himself "because daily I expect death as a heretic."⁵⁰ But in a visit with his father, Hans, who had resented Luther's going into the monastery precisely because that meant he would never marry and have children, and who now implored him for a grandson. It also came into Luther's mind that if he were to get married, this would be a good way to throw his freedom into the face of his critics.

Finally, he made his decision: "If I can arrange it, I will marry Kate in defiance of the devil and all his adversaries."⁵¹ After praying about it, he came up with a "battery of reasons in favor of his proposal: his marriage would please his father, rile the pope, cause the angels to laugh and the devils to weep."⁵²

They got married. Luther had no money or place to live to start a family. He still lived in the monastery. Wedding gifts poured in, including gifts of cash, which helped. Elector John came to the rescue, essentially giving the monastery (which no longer housed any monks) and its grounds to the Luthers, as well as a salary of two hundred gulden per year.

That was a modest middle-class income. Luther still refused to take any money for his Bible and his writings. The city, which did not have to pay its preacher, chipped in with semiregular gifts of produce, cloth, and other supplies. But money was always tight. One problem was Luther's habit of always giving it away.

Kate, or Katie, as Luther called her, took over the management of the household. She supplemented their family income by gardening and tending fruit trees. She raised chickens, geese, pigs, cows, and bees. She even brewed beer.

The monastery had been called "the Black Cloister," which she must have found depressing, so she had it painted white. She remodeled the building, breaking up the constricted cells into rooms for a family.

She found that he had been sleeping on straw that had not been changed for years, a situation she remedied with a proper bed. She took care of her husband, which he tended not to do for himself, seeing that he was properly dressed, tending to his health, and making sure he was fed. She fattened him up, and Luther's former gauntness gave way to the bulk usually associated with him.

Their relationship grew and deepened, becoming a model of marital love. Keep in mind that marriage up to this time had been denigrated. The church had seen marriage as a concession for the weak and the need to procreate, but it was unworthy of those who wished to be truly spiritual. The culture often treated marriage in terms of property acquisition, with the wife being valued for the property she brought into the family and often as a piece of property herself.

The Luthers, though, became role models for the high view of marriage that was gradually taking hold, thanks to the Reformation. Their marriage was in public view, thanks in part to the large number of people they took into their home and the constant stream of visitors they entertained. Luther, to be sure, was the head of the house, but Kate was a strong woman in her own right, and the two became true partners.

In his letters to her, we see their deep affection. They tease each other, and they support each other emotionally and spiritually.

"Kate, my rib, greets you," Luther wrote a friend after his first year of marriage, "whom, in my poverty, I would not exchange for all the wealth of Croesus."[53] He said he would not trade her for France or Venice. He called her an empress, a theologian, a gift of God.

They had their first child on June 7, 1526. Luther was a tender father to little Hans. He would put him to bed with words like a lullaby: "Go now and be godly. No money will I leave you, but a rich God I will leave you. Only be godly."[54]

A daughter, Elizabeth, was born in 1527. She died eight months later. The parents were heartbroken. With her death, he wrote, "Died a piece of her father's and a part of her mother's heart."[55] In 1529 another daughter was born, Magdalene. Her parents doted on her, but she died at just over one year old. Martin was born on November 9, 1531. Paul on January 29, 1533. Then another daughter, Margarete, just before Christmas in 1534.

Luther's *Table Talk,* the transcripts of the dinner conversations among the Luthers and their numerous guests, records many priceless anecdotes about the couple. As an example of their repartee, Luther once was giving Katie a hard time. "One of these days a man will have more than one wife," he said.

"Only the devil would accept that as true," Kate replied. She quoted Paul, the scripture about how a leader in the church should be the husband of one wife.

"True," said Luther, "but not *just* one."

"If that happens," she said, "I will leave you with all the children and return to the nunnery."[56]

One day Luther was lost in one of his bleak, nearly despairing moods. Kate put on a black dress. Luther soon asked, "Are you going to a funeral?" "No," she replied, "but since you act as though God is dead, I wanted to join you in your mourning." Luther got the point and pulled out of his depression.[57]

Revolution

*A*BOUT THE SAME TIME that Luther was dealing with Erasmus, a different theological controversy was manifesting itself in violence, fanaticism, and anarchy. As the Reformation spread geographically among the common people, what had happened in Wittenberg to bring Luther out of hiding broke out elsewhere.

Andreas Karlstadt left Wittenberg for the countryside and brought his new theology with him. The Zwickau prophets traveled from village to village as they kept being expelled by the authorities. One of them was a firebrand preacher named Thomas Müntzer.

The theology of Karlstadt and Müntzer is called "enthusiasm," from Greek words meaning "God inside." They believed the Holy Spirit dwells inside Christians and speaks to them and through them. This is similar to today's charismatic theology, but these two took the idea much further, to the point of saying that the Bible, the external Word, is not necessary.

Then Müntzer really went off the deep end. He said that these are the last days when true Christians will rise up and rule the earth. He said that the ungodly should be slain. He told the peasants to rise up, kill their masters, eliminate all property, own everything in common, and establish a utopian millennial age before Christ's Second Coming. "Look not," he said, "on the sorrow of the ungodly; let not your sword grow cold from blood; strike hard upon the anvil of Nimrod [that is, the princes]; cast his tower to the ground, because the day is yours."[58]

The peasants had legitimate grievances. They were terribly used and oppressed. Luther had urged the princes and the feudal lords of the manors to lower the taxes and improve the conditions. But Müntzer's inflammatory rhetoric—which anticipated the communist revolution by four centuries—was like throwing a lighted match into dry brush.

The peasants who heard Müntzer were uneducated and theologically naive, yet they were filled with a sense of freedom from the gospel. The old oppressive religious structures were thrown off. Why not the old oppressive social structures as well?

What became known as the Peasants' War broke out in the summer of 1524 in Swabia, right next to Switzerland. It spread through central and southwestern Germany. Mobs of peasants rose up against the landowners, killing their former masters and their families, burning farms and homes. Peasant armies destroyed castles and palaces of the princes and sometimes defeated organized armies sent to put down the rebellion.[59]

The revolt spread into Catholic lands as well—which the Catholics, of course, blamed on Luther and the effects of his teachings—and the peasants poured out their wrath in particular on bishops, priests, monks, and nuns. "Every day," reported Erasmus, "priests are imprisoned, tortured, hanged, decapitated, or burnt."[60]

Luther preached and wrote against the theology of enthusiasm. Müntzer and his fellow prophets were no different than the pope, he pointed out. Both believe the Holy Spirit speaks to them apart from the Word. Actually, the enthusiasts are worse. The Catholics have only one pope. With the enthusiasts, everyone is a pope.

Luther also attacked the enthusiasts' project of seizing earthly power and setting up the perfect society on earth. Christ's kingdom is not of this world, and He—not sinful human beings—will establish it. God rules in the spiritual kingdom through His Word, but He rules in His earthly kingdom, as Romans 13 shows, through the secular government. Rebellion against the lawful authorities is a sin, and the dream of fallen human beings ever establishing a perfect society on earth is an illusion.

Luther tried to mediate between the nobility and the peasants, who trusted him (though Müntzer said he hated Luther worse than the pope). Luther wrote a book, *Admonition to Peace.* But the violence only increased. Whole provinces fell into anarchy.

So Luther wrote another book, *Against the Raging Peasants,* addressed to the princes. The church wields the Word, but, he reminded them, the secular rulers wield the sword. God has given them the authority to keep the peace and establish social order, and Romans 13 warns rulers not to bear the sword in vain. This is the vocation, the divine calling, of a Christian prince. In the face of anarchy, he said, rulers must use any force necessary.

"Therefore let everyone who can, smite, slay, and stab," Luther told the princes, turning his harsh rhetoric against the rebelling peasants, "remembering that nothing can be more poisonous, hurtful, or devilish than a rebel. It is just as when one must kill a mad dog; if you do not strike him, he will strike you, and the whole land with you."[61]

And so the princes did. Elector John joined forces with Philip of Hesse, Duke Henry of Brunswick, and other rulers, both evangelical and Catholic. They met the peasant army at Frankenhausen on May 25, 1525, and killed five thousand. Three hundred more were captured and beheaded. Müntzer was captured, tortured, and executed. The Catholic forces of the emperor slaughtered the rebels in southern Germany. In Alsace eighteen thousand peasants fell.[62]

An estimated one hundred thousand peasants were killed.[63] They, in turn, had burned more than a thousand castles and convents. Hundreds of villages were destroyed. What were once vast farmlands had been laid waste, the cattle killed and the land turned back into wilderness.[64]

Luther himself was horrified. Many peasants who had once looked to him with gratitude now turned against him and his theology. Luther was attacked from both sides. Catholics blamed the revolution on him, saying, in effect, See what Luther's ideas lead to? Erasmus and other humanists blamed Luther's harsh writings for the cruelty of the princes' response. As if the princes would have accepted losing their realms to anarchy, and as if they would not have acted on their own soon enough.

Luther published *An Open Letter on the Harsh Book Against the Peasants* in which he defended his basic position while urging the princes to show mercy and not take revenge against the defeated peasants, nor set themselves up as tyrants.

On June 27, 1524, Luther and Katie's wedding night, who should show up at their door but Andreas Karlstadt. He had taken part in the Peasants' War as a rebel and was now in a state of abject poverty. He came to Luther and repented. He recanted his last books. He promised never to write, teach, or preach again. He apologized to Wittenberg for the unrest he caused. He repudiated the Peasants' War.

Luther took him in, an act of loving and forgiving his enemy. Karlstadt stayed with Luther and Katie for eight weeks. At first, this was in secret, since Luther did not want the elector to know that Karlstadt was there lest he be arrested. Later, Luther interceded for him with the elector, who allowed Karlstadt to take up farming again. And yet Luther would still have to contend with the ideas of his old adversary.

TEACHING THE PEOPLE

*W*HILE MUCH PROGRESS HAD been made Reforming the church, Luther and his colleagues realized that much of it was from the top down.
Attention needed to be paid to the grass roots, to the far-
flung local congregations, and to the spiritual lives of the
common people. If the peasants were so susceptible to
the rabble-rousing prophets, they were obviously in severe need of solid biblical instruction.

The first step was to assess where things stood. With
the cooperation of Elector John, who gave them the
needed authority, the Wittenberg theologians organized a
"visitation" of all the Saxon congregations.

The concern was for both the spiritual and the economic well-being of each church. Under Rome, churches
exacted exorbitant taxes, exploiting the people, who
would be excommunicated if they failed to pay what they
owed. All of that was gone. So now many people were
not giving *anything* to the church.

In 1526 the visitations began and lasted two years. The
teams consisted of two laypeople qualified to look at the

church's finances, two educators to evaluate the quality of the local schools, and two theologians who quizzed the pastors on their knowledge of the Bible and assessed the faith and morals of the members.

When the results of the visitations were made known, the news was not good. The congregations' finances were a shambles. Many of the schools were terrible. In an embarrassingly large number of cases, the pastors were uneducated and theologically ignorant. As for the people, immorality was rampant. Many of them thought the gospel and the end of the Roman rituals simply meant they could do whatever they wanted.

To remedy the situation, the elector appropriated the monastic lands and the vast wealth of the Roman Church in Saxony to help support the local congregations. Melanchthon devised a rigorous classical curriculum for the schools. And Luther composed his greatest contribution to Christian education, a work that has been used from generation to generation to teach the basic tenets of Christianity to millions to this day: the Small Catechism.

Historically, the catechism consisted of three texts that were used to teach the basics of the Christian faith: the Ten Commandments; the Lord's Prayer; and the Apostles' Creed. Then questions and explanations would help the students to understand what they mean.

Luther's catechism could be used for the instruction of children and adults alike. It was designed to be used by families as well as by pastors, giving biblical truths "as the head of the family should teach them in a simple way to his household."[65]

Luther's method of Christian education followed the techniques of classical education, the *trivium:* (1) learning the basics by heart (grammar), (2) understanding them, by means of dialectical questions answering "What does this mean?"(logic), and (3) adopting and confessing them before the church (rhetoric). The language of the catechism was simple, succinct, eloquent, and profound.

Thus, in the treatment of the Ten Commandments, Luther gave the Scripture. Then he applied it, as Christ did, to the attitudes of the heart. He also related the commandment to love God and love one's neighbor, which Christ said is the sum of all the law and the prophets (Matthew 22:37–40). He explained the commandment in terms of what we are *not* to do and also what we *are* to do. All in a single graceful sentence.

> Thou shalt not kill.
> *What does this mean?* We should fear and love God that we may not hurt nor harm our neighbor in his body, but help and befriend him in every bodily need.

> Thou shalt not bear false witness against thy neighbor.
> *What does this mean?* We should fear and love God that we may not deceitfully belie, betray, slander, nor defame our neighbor, but defend him, speak well of him, and put the best construction on everything.[66]

The law is followed by the gospel, which is the theme of the Trinitarian teaching of the Apostles' Creed. For a sampling, here is the explanation of the second article, "I believe . . . in Jesus Christ":

What does this mean? I believe that Jesus Christ, true God, begotten of the Father from eternity, and also true man, born of the Virgin Mary, is my Lord,

who has redeemed me, a lost and condemned creature, purchased and won me from all sins, from death, and from the power of the devil; not with gold or silver, but with His holy, precious blood and with His innocent suffering and death,

that I may be His own, and live under Him in His kingdom, and serve Him in everlasting righteousness, innocence, and blessedness,

even as He is risen from the dead, lives and reigns to all eternity.

This is most certainly true.[67]

The law, the gospel, then the relationship with God through Jesus Christ, which Luther shows by unfolding the Lord's Prayer:

Our Father who art in heaven.

What does this mean? God would by these words tenderly invite us to believe that He is our true Father, and that we are His true children, so that we may with all boldness and confidence ask Him as dear children ask their dear father.

Also in Luther's Small Catechism are sections on baptism, the confession of sins, and the Lord's Supper, along with model prayers for morning, evening, and meals. The final section is the Table of Duties, which conveys his doctrine of vocation. It consists of the Bible verses that set forth what God asks of pastors and members of the congregation, rulers and subjects, husbands and wives, parents and children, employers and workers, widows and young people. Underpinning these teachings is the law of love for everyone.

The Small Catechism came out in 1529. Also that year he published the Large Catechism, derived mostly from his sermons, which was designed to go into more depth for the instruction of pastors and teachers.

Luther also wrote his *Church Postils,* a series of sermons for the church year to be used as samples for pastors. Those who lacked the ability to preach sermons on their own were instructed to simply read Luther's to their congregations.

Another powerful tool in shaping the piety of the people was Luther's music. One of the innovations in the Reformation worship service was congregational singing. Before, only the choir and the priests would chant the Psalms, liturgical set pieces, and Latin hymns. The Middle Ages did have some popular religious songs in the language of the people, but they were mostly devoted to saints and the Virgin Mary. Luther wanted the people to sing in their worship, so there was a need for solid, biblical, evangelical hymns.

Another of Luther's multitudinous gifts was music. He could play the lute, and he was said to have had a fine tenor voice. And of course, his mastery of language made him an extraordinarily good poet. So he started writing hymns. Others did too, so that the time was a golden age in the history of church music. But Luther's were among the strongest and the best loved.

Luther wrote thirty-seven hymns. The first, as we have seen, was in 1523, soon after he had finished translating the New Testament, upon hearing of the first of many who were martyred for the gospel. He wrote twenty-one hymns in 1524. His last two were written in 1543, three years before he died.[68]

It is often said that Luther took bar tunes from the taverns to use with his hymns. This is a rather comical misunderstanding of the technical term "bar-form," which refers to a particular kind of phrase structure in a piece of music. Musicologists do note that Luther used the bar-form in his music, but that does not mean what some people think it does. He sometimes arranged tunes derived from Gregorian chant, folk songs, and medieval hymns, but often he composed music that was completely original.[69]

We will discuss his music further—including his most famous hymn, "A Mighty Fortress"—in the last section of this book, on Luther's "legacy." For now, we will stress that the problems uncovered in the visitations were thoroughly and effectively addressed. Luther's hymns played an important role, along with his catechisms and his Bible (once the people were taught how to read it), in shaping the piety of generations of ordinary Christians.

SPLIT WITH THE REFORMED

*A*S THE REFORMATION GREW, other theologians made contributions of their own, with significant differences from Luther. These hinged particularly on their understanding of the sacraments. The enthusiasts had also differed with Luther on the sacraments, but more sophisticated theologians started teaching the same thing.

Andreas Karlstadt and the enthusiasts had also questioned baptismal regeneration and the baptism of infants. They also rejected the presence of Christ in the bread and wine of Holy Communion. Luther believed that both baptism and the Lord's Supper are "means of grace," in which the Holy Spirit and Christ Himself are present, conveying forgiveness and creating faith. The different views on these and other issues would serve as the basis for the various Protestant traditions and denominations that exist to this day. At the time, though, these differences threatened to tear the Reformation apart and to put the Roman Catholic Church back in power.

The so-called Sacramentarians—which meant, ironically, those who did *not* have Luther's high view of the sacraments—were all, at first, humanists who converted to the evangelical cause. The most important was Ulrich Zwingli, an early opponent of indulgences and abuses in the church. He began his work just a few years after Luther posted his theses, so that his theology developed separately. Zwingli carried out his reforms in Zurich, Switzerland, and attracted followers of his own, such as John Oecolampadius, a professor at the University of Basel.

Zwingli taught that the Lord's Supper was a symbolic memorial meal. He threw out the liturgy completely in favor of a simple service of preaching, rejecting not only all religious images but even music. The Bible, for him, was a rule book for all of life, and nothing that was not specified in Scripture would be permitted in the church or in the city itself. Celebrations of the old holidays and festivals of the church year were forbidden.

Martin Bucer and Wolfgang Capito were at first in Luther's camp but then became convinced by Zwingli's writings, as did others throughout Germany. Karlstadt, of course, had come to similar conclusions in his days as a theologian before lapsing into complete enthusiasm. Even after his repentance, his writings remained influential.

The controversy ignited into a firestorm when Bucer translated a commentary on the Psalms by Bugenhagen, the pastor of the Wittenberg church. But Bucer changed what Bugenhagen said, putting words into his mouth to make him say that the Lord's Supper was purely a memorial meal. Then, when Bucer did a Latin translation of Luther's Lenten sermons, he did the same thing to Luther!

Luther blasted back at Bucer with *The Sacrament of the Body and Blood of Christ—Against the Fanatics* (1526). Bucer arranged for Zwingli to answer for him, with a friendly sounding but actually condescending tract entitled *Friendly Exposition of the Eucharist Affair, to [Not Against] Martin Luther.* This was answered by Luther's *That These Words of Christ "This is my Body," etc., Still Stand Firm Against the Fanatics* (1527). And on and on, into an ever-escalating war of words on both sides.

As all of this was going on, with evangelicals becoming more and more polarized as they followed the debate and took one position or the other, the emperor was preparing to enforce the Edict of Worms.

After the confrontation in Worms, the diet met again the next year at Nuremberg. There was a new pope, Hadrian VI, who made the significant admission that the church was responsible for abuses but demanded that the Edict of Worms be enforced. The diet ruled, though, that it was impossible at that time to enforce the ban and called for a general church council to settle the issues.

For a time the emperor was distracted by a war with France. And then a war with the pope! But a number of Catholic principalities were organizing themselves as the Regensburg League with the purpose of forming a military alliance to quash the Reformation. In 1529 the Diet of Speyer called for the Edict of Worms to be enforced.

The evangelical princes, led by Philip of Hesse, felt impelled to form their own league to defend against this threat. But the Reformation had split into factions over the Sacramentarian controversy, and its members were at each other's throats. The princes wanted these questions resolved. They felt it was of the utmost urgency to restore unity. Otherwise, despite all that had happened, the Church of Rome might squelch the Reformation once and for all.

Philip called for a colloquy—a formal conversation—be held at Marburg for the purpose of coming to an agreement. On September 30, 1529, the Marburg Colloquy began. Its structure provided for Luther to have a discussion with Oecolampadius while Melanchthon had a discussion with Zwingli. (The idea was to keep the two principle opponents away from each other at first.) Then all four would meet together for a plenary discussion. In attendance would be theologians, professors, pastors, and court officials representing Reformation states throughout the empire.

The plenary discussion began on October 2 and went on for three days. Luther insisted on accepting the plain words of Scripture. He did not believe in transubstantiation, the Roman Catholic notion that the bread and wine change into Christ's body and blood, only appearing to be bread and wine. He did not accept other metaphysical accounts, including "consubstantiation"—though this view is often ascribed to him—according to which the elements have two different substances.

Luther believed that the bread remains bread and yet, by the power of the Word of God as spoken in the words of institution, Christ's body is spiritually but objectively present "in, with, and under" the bread. His blood is present in the wine so that the sacrament bestows the gospel—the forgiveness of sins through Christ's broken body and spilled blood—which is received by faith.

His objection to Zwingli was that he was following human reason instead of the Word of God, that he insisted on interpreting away what the Word of God said. He felt Zwingli kept trying to give rationalistic explanations not only for the words of institution but for the other passages—such as the text that speaks of the bread and wine being "a participation" in the body and blood of Christ (1 Corinthians 10:16–17) and the text that speaks about the sacrament being received not just by the faithful but by the unworthy, who profane the body of Christ and thus receive it to their condemnation (1 Corinthians 11:27), which implies that Christ's body is objectively present and not just received spiritually by the faithful.

Zwingli kept trying to *interpret* the Bible, insisting on making it say something more comprehensible than what it actually did say. In general, Luther was against interpretation, which he felt was a pretext for human reason to seize authority over the Word of God in all its mystery. One could set verses next to each other, use Scripture to explain Scripture, think about, and apply Scripture, but he was against "interpretation," insisting that each verse of the Bible, whether we understand it or not, be accepted on its own terms.

Many people today may disagree with Luther on this as well as other issues. But this is a biography. Its purpose is to understand the man. Luther was motivated at every point by a rigorous, uncompromising, and unyielding adherence to the Word of God. And the Marburg Colloquy shows us the quintessential Luther in a way second only to his stand against a very different opponent at the Diet of Worms.

During the plenary discussion, Luther took a piece of chalk and wrote on the table in large letters, "THIS IS MY BODY." When Zwingli would launch into his explanations of what he thought the Lord's Supper meant, Luther would just point to those words.

The picture it calls to mind is rather comical, but—agree or disagree on the issues—imagining the scene gives us the unwatered-down Luther. "Well, what the gospel-writers really intended by those words is . . ." THIS IS MY BODY. "Yes, of course, Dr. Luther, but this clearly has to be a metaphorical construction . . ." THIS IS MY BODY. "But surely you will have to admit that Christ's body was taken up to heaven so that now . . ." THIS IS MY BODY.

As far as Luther was concerned, it was not up to him to spin out a theory. He would be silent. He would let the Word of God speak. On those particular words from Scripture, he would stand.

Not only that, he would stand on the Word of God no matter the consequences. For every pragmatic and political and practical reason, it was essential that the evangelicals should stop their squabbling and unite. But Luther would rather the movement he himself started be destroyed than give up or compromise a single verse from Scripture.

At a time when the Regensburg League might sweep them all and do to the evangelicals what those same princes had already done to the peasants, at a time when the emperor was threatening to bring to bear his whole power and might to stamp out the Reformation completely—possibilities that were in the back of the mind of everyone at Marburg—Luther refused to back down from his convictions. In his mind, they were not his convictions but the Word of God. THIS IS MY BODY.

The exasperated Philip of Hesse asked Luther and Zwingli what they *could* agree on. They made a list. Their areas of agreement were considerable. Original sin. The two natures of Christ. Justification by faith.

They had earlier agreed that ceremonies would be considered matters of Christian freedom. Luther did not insist on the liturgy as such, or that everyone had to worship in exactly the same way. When five years later the Church of England would be founded, the Anglican tradition would allow for wide differences of doctrine as long as everyone followed the same order of worship. The Lutherans would take the opposite approach, allowing different orders of worship as long as everyone agreed on doctrine. It should be stressed, though, that, for Luther and his followers, making ceremonies a matter of freedom meant *the freedom to have them.* It was Zwingli and his followers who would not even allow an organ in church, rejecting all ceremonies that might also have been used in the Church of Rome, including those that had an evangelical meaning and that pointed to Christ. But Luther did not care whether or not Zwingli used an organ. He just wanted him to have a higher view of the sacraments.

The parties signed what would be called the Marburg Articles, which included a statement that they could not agree on the Lord's Supper but that they further agreed to be friends and to help one another in times of need.

Just as the meeting was ending, Bucer asked Luther, Don't you accept me as an orthodox Christian? Luther replied, "You have a different spirit than ours."[70]

This hurt Bucer and Zwingli deeply. We agree on the essentials. Why make such a divisive issue out of a secondary matter of far lesser importance? But that they thought the sacrament was relatively unimportant was the whole problem, as far as Luther was concerned. Indeed, to this day, it is hard for other Protestants to realize just how important Holy Communion is to Lutherans, what a central role it plays in the spirituality and in the experiential piety of Lutheran laypeople.

Although Luther referred to a different spirit, he did not imply that the Zwinglians did not have the *Holy Spirit,* that they were not Christians. After all, both groups had just signed the papers agreeing on justification. Instead he believed Lutherans and Zwinglians had a different spirit in the sense of a different approach to the Christian life, a different spiritual sensibility.

As Luther saw it, Zwingli was using the Bible as a law book, emphasizing its dos and don'ts, whereas Luther saw the Bible in terms of the gospel, as opening up Christian freedom. While the Zwinglians were busy banning Christmas, getting political power over Zurich, and enforcing public morals, Luther—who never had the stereotypical "puritan" mentality—viewed them as too moralistic, even legalistic. They seemed closer to the Roman Catholics he had been battling. In Zwingli's dependence on reason, he seemed too much like the humanists. In rejecting the sacraments as an objective means of grace in favor of a purely inward spiritual illumination, he seemed too much like the enthusiasts.

At any rate, after the Marburg Colloquy, the Reformation branched off into two directions. It would thereafter be possible to distinguish between the "Reformed" and the "Evangelical" (the name Luther preferred, which eventually would give way to "Lutheran").[71] At the time of the colloquy, a twenty-year-old Frenchman named John Calvin had just started his career as a lawyer. Six years later he would write *The Institutes* and become the greatest theologian of the Reformed branch of the Reformation. Two years after the colloquy, Zwingli would be killed in battle, fighting the Swiss Catholics.

ISLAMIC JIHAD

*L*OOMING OVER THE CONFLICTS within Christendom, beginning about the time of Luther's posting of his theses and intensifying two decades later, was a threat of global and cultural proportions: Islam.[72]

Throughout the history of Western civilization, it has periodically been attacked by militant Islam. Toward the end of the Dark Ages, that unsettled time after the fall of Rome, Muslim conquerors swept through North Africa, conquered Spain, and were poised to overrun all of Europe until they were defeated by Charles "the Hammer" Martel just outside Paris at the battle of Tours (732). During the Middle Ages, the West invaded Muslim lands in the Crusades. Now it was happening again as the emperor of Turkey, Sulayman the Magnificent, commanding vast armies and absolute power, went on *jihad* to spread Islam with the sword.

Today the West is once again in a life-and-death struggle with radical Islamic groups. The main difference is that today the West is superior militarily, economically, and culturally, so that the jihadists have to resort to terrorism. But in the sixteenth century, the Muslims were arguably superior to the Europeans militarily, economically, and if not culturally, at least politically, as the emperors of the Ottoman dynasty exercised absolute power in their realms, in striking contrast to the decentralized, fractured principalities of Europe. For those who believe in political freedom, the Western model, of course, is much better, but in fighting a massive war, the Ottomans' absolutism gave them some short-term advantages.

The Ottoman Empire began in Turkey as Muslims overthrew the ancient Christian city of Constantinople in 1453. Much of Persia, Syria, and Arabia were brought into the empire, then Egypt and the northern rim of Africa along the Mediterranean Sea. Then the Muslim armies moved north into parts of Russia (today's Chechens are a remnant of those days), then west. Greece, the cradle of Western civilization, fell. So did the Balkans (today's Bosnians are the descendants of the Serbs who embraced Islam), as well as Bulgaria, Romania, and Hungary. By the first decades of the sixteenth century the Turks were on the borders of Austria and Germany, and they were getting ready to invade.

From the Holy Roman emperor's point of view, this was the very worst time for a theological dispute. He had to defend Christendom from the forces of Islam. This was a time when Christians needed to unify against a common foe. The pope, meanwhile, responded by calling a crusade, complete with indulgences for those who died defending Europe from the Muslim invader.

As early as 1518 Luther was preaching and writing against the crusade. Luther opposed any kind of Christian jihad that promised everlasting life for the good work of dying while killing the enemies of God (precisely what today's Islamic terrorists believe). Again, against all expediency and pragmatism, even though the Turks might swoop down and wipe out Christianity altogether, Luther refused to compromise the Word of God. Again, he was standing on the gospel.

Implicit in the gospel is the trust that *God acts.* God will protect Christianity, Luther said. The Turk is a scourge of God to punish us for our sins and to force us to depend on Him instead of on ourselves. But there can be no holy war as far as Christians are concerned.

Then, developing his doctrines of vocation and of the two kingdoms, Luther said that it was the calling of the secular rulers to defend their people. This is the task of the emperor and the princes. This is also part of the calling of Christian soldiers, to love and serve their neighbors by fighting on their behalf.

One reason that the emperor treated the evangelical princes with such forbearance was that he needed them to help fend off the Turks. Thus, ironically, the Islamic invasion may have helped make the Reformation possible.

Luther would write six books on Islam, including a preface to the Koran.[73] A theme of his theological critiques of Islam was that, like that of the pope, it is a religion of the law only, seeing salvation only in terms of human works, with no gospel of forgiveness.

The Turkish threat grew greater with each year. And the situation was getting desperate. By 1529, at the time Luther and Zwingli were arguing at Marburg, the Turks laid siege to Vienna.[74]

HERE WE STAND

*E*MPEROR CHARLES V SUMMONED the diet to appear at Augsburg on June 20, 1530. This would be the first diet since that of Worms over which the emperor would preside in person. For the past nine years, in the other diets, he had sent a representative, so entangled was he with problems in Spain, a war with France, and a war with the pope, in which his men had actually sacked Rome. He made peace with the pope, who crowned him emperor. Those matters finally settled, Charles resolved to solve, once and for all, the problem of religious division and organize the princes to mobilize against the Turks.

Elector John told the Wittenberg theologians to draw up a confession of faith to show the emperor what the evangelical princes believed in the hope that he might prove tolerant. Luther assigned the task to Melanchthon, who drew up a confession of faith that clearly expressed the evangelical beliefs, while, at the same time, demonstrated their "catholicity," their continuity with historic Christianity. One can only imagine its tone if Luther had written it, but Melanchthon, being diplomatic and peace-loving, as well as being a superb theologian, struck just the right note. To this day the Augsburg Confession is the foundational doctrinal statement of Lutheranism to which all pastors and teachers must subscribe.

Seven princes and the representatives of two imperial cities signed the Augsburg Confession and resolved to present it to the emperor. Elector John wanted Luther nearby for consultations, even though he would be under the ban and subject to arrest if he appeared in Augsburg. So once again an elector of Saxony ensconced Luther in disguise in a castle, this time at Coburg on the very far-flung border of his realm, just inside the safety of Saxony but not far from Augsburg. Luther was accompanied by his friend and secretary, Veit Dietrich.

In Augsburg the diet was to begin with an elaborate *Corpus Christi* procession, a Roman Catholic ceremony with all the trimmings. The evangelical princes refused to join in. The emperor also banned all evangelical preaching in the city, but the princes held their worship service in private houses. When the emperor challenged them on this behavior, Margrave George of Brandenburg said he would rather lose his head than deny God. The emperor, apparently moved by his faithfulness, replied in his broken German, "Dear prince, not head off, not head off."[75]

On June 25, 1525, the Augsburg Confession was presented to the emperor and read before the diet. Many on the Catholic side were surprised to hear what the evangelicals actually believed, since this statement, beginning with the acceptance of the ancient creeds and briefly making the scriptural case for the gospel, was not nearly as wild and fanatical as their advisers had told them. The bishop of Augsburg was heard to say that it was the pure truth. Duke William of Bavaria lambasted John Eck, Luther's old adversary, who was present, for misrepresenting what the Lutherans believed. Eck said he could refute it, not with the Bible, but with the church fathers. "I am to understand, then," asked the duke, "that the Lutherans are within the Scriptures, and we Catholics on the outside?"[76]

The emperor referred the Augsburg Confession to a committee of theologians, including Eck, who quickly came out with a document refuting it. Melanchthon came back with a thorough defense, the Apology of the Augsburg Confession, which would also become an authoritative Lutheran confession of faith.

But the emperor declared the Augsburg Confession refuted and would not receive Melanchthon's refutation of the refutation. Melanchthon, fearing the worst, plunged into behind-the-scenes negotiations with the pope's representative—who was advocating bringing the Spanish Inquisition into Germany—seeing what concessions might keep the peace. At first Melanchthon worried that the confession he wrote was too mild, and now he worried that it was too harsh. He was depressed and desperate. He kept writing Luther to see what he should do.

From Coburg, Luther told him to stand firm and not to worry. Everything is in the hands of God, he kept saying. Sit back. God will act. In the meantime, while in Coburg, Luther wrote and prayed.

The emperor declared that the old faith must be restored. No more evangelical writings were to be published.

He would urge the pope to declare a council to work out the religious questions, but in the meantime the Edict of Worms would be in force. The emperor gave the evangelical princes until April 15, 1531, a period of about seven months, to reconsider their position. After that, he said, they could expect the emperor to take forcible action against them.

Soon after, the princes formed a defensive alliance for military action, the Smalcald League, open to anyone who would subscribe to the Augsburg Confession. But was it legitimate to resist the emperor? Luther had always said that it was not, and characteristically, he did not take back his position despite what it would mean for himself and his cause. The court lawyers, though, found that the emperor had no legal right to wage war on his own people. The case was made that the rulers of each state received their authority from God and that the emperor received his authority from them, since they elected him. Thus they asserted what, in the centuries ahead, would have huge ramifications for political freedom: parliamentary authority over the monarch. Luther grudgingly accepted that local rulers had the right to defend their people when they were attacked, insisting too that the emperor had no right to overrule the gospel.

But as both sides were making preparations for war, suddenly peace broke out. In April 1532 Sulayman launched a new invasion with a force of three hundred thousand. The emperor did not want to fight the evangelicals. He needed them for the war against the Turks.

The emperor called another diet at Nuremberg that same month and declared a temporary peace. The pope would declare a council. In the meantime, there would be religious toleration for six years on condition that the evangelical princes would join with the emperor in fighting the Turks. They did. The Turks were defeated. Christendom was saved after all.

At the Diet of Worms, Luther had stood before the emperor and the members of the diet, confessing his faith, all alone and at the risk of his life. Four years later at the Diet of Augsburg, not he, but rulers representing thousands of others who likewise had come to know the gospel through the Word of God, were making that same confession before the same audience. They were saying, in effect, Here we stand.

HIS DECLINE

*D*URING THE PEACE OF Nuremberg, the Reformation had six years to catch its breath and get back on track. Soon after the peace had been declared, Elector John the Steadfast died. He was succeeded by John Frederick the Magnanimous, a devout evangelical. The diplomatic and political intrigues continued.

Luther settled into family life. He and Katie had their last two children, Paul being born in 1533 and Margarete in 1534. The Luthers, living in that big former monastery, kept boarders, particularly university students. Their hospitality to the students, their friends, and a constant stream of visitors was legendary, as was the conversation at the dinner table. Beginning in 1531 and continuing almost to his death, Veit Dietrich and a succession of others began taking notes on the things Luther said over dinner, which turned into the treasure trove of wit and profundity that was published as *The Table Talk.*

Luther kept preaching and would do so until the Sunday before he died. He kept writing. He resumed his work at the university, lecturing on the Bible. These lectures, some of which were recorded by Dietrich, were later published as commentaries. They contain some of his most penetrating theological insights. In 1535 he was made dean of the theology faculty at the university, piling administrative responsibilities onto him.

As the Reformation continued to spread, people continued to consult with Luther on how to reform their churches. Princes kept asking him what they should do, and so did his friends and neighbors.

Luther continued to deal with theological controversies. In 1534 he had to deal with the Anabaptist movement, which taught that only adults should be baptized since only adults can have faith. Luther maintained that little children too can have faith. Just as an infant can love and trust his mother and father, an infant can love and trust Jesus, who lifted up infants as the model for the faith of adults. Faith is not the assent of the will, nor intellectual understanding. Rather, he believed, it is a gift of God, created by the Holy Spirit, who works through baptism.

The emperor had asked the pope to call a general council to resolve the issues once and for all. The pope said he would but kept delaying. Luther expected a church council to do little good, but the princes believed they would be safe in the meantime. In 1537 the Smalcald League asked Luther to prepare another confession of faith if ever a council should be called, which he did. The original purpose was to state the issues in which the evangelicals would be willing to compromise, and the answer was "not at all." The Smalcald Articles went further than the Augsburg Confession, going on to reject the papacy, deny the existence of purgatory, and define the Roman abuses more sharply. The Smalcald Articles became another official Lutheran confession of faith.

In 1538 Luther had to deal with a false theology that came right out of Wittenberg. One of his former students, John Agricola, began teaching what Luther's enemies had always falsely accused him of teaching: antinomianism, that since Christians are saved by grace, there is no need for any moral laws.

Luther had to correct this misunderstanding by developing the proper distinction between law and gospel. There are three uses of the law: (1) to restrain evil in the secular sphere, to make it possible for sinful human beings to live together in a society, (2) to convict our heart so that we can see ourselves as sinners and so repent and turn to Christ, (3) to guide Christians in God's will so that they freely live in a way pleasing to Him. Christians need to keep hearing God's law, just as they need to keep hearing Christ's gospel, since, as he said in the first of his theses that began the Reformation, "When our Lord and Master, Jesus Christ, said 'Repent,' He called for the entire life of believers to be one of penitence."

But after 1537, as Martin Brecht puts it, Luther was "ill, old, and tired of living."[77] He was only in his fifties, but this was already a long life in those days. All of his life he struggled with health problems, but now they grew worse. He had circulatory problems that gave him fainting spells. He was prone to intense headaches. He had kidney stones. He had bouts of incapacitating exhaustion. He was growing frailer.

Worst of all, his powers were failing him. A particularly embarrassing incident happened in 1539 when Philip of

Hesse asked Luther and Melanchthon if he could have two wives. Philip was in an unhappy marriage and fell in love with a seventeen-year-old lady-in-waiting. He made the young woman his mistress, but his conscience was tormenting him to the point that he was afraid to take Holy Communion. He recognized that his soul was in danger. He did not want to be committing adultery. At the same time, he just could not give her up. Couldn't he just marry her? Yes, that would be bigamy, but the patriarchs in the Bible had more than one wives, so how bad could that be?

Luther and Melanchthon were taken aback at this. They counseled him. They admonished him. Finally, they determined that the Bible did not explicitly forbid bigamy and having two wives would be better than committing adultery. They told him, however, not to make this public, since it would be a terrible example to others, and this unusual exception must not become a generally accepted practice. Under the seal and the secrecy of confession, they gave him dispensation to marry the girl. So Philip had two wives. But no one was to know.

Of course, the rumors flew and the gossip spread like wildfire. Finally, Philip admitted it. He said that Luther and Melanchthon had approved and had recommended this action. Rome used this as an example of the shocking immorality that always accompanied the Reformation. The scandal was a fiasco. Luther admitted that letting Philip take a second wife was one of the biggest mistakes of his life. The only thing that can be said in their defense is that neither Philip nor Luther nor Melanchthon even considered Henry VIII's solution: divorcing the first wife.

Though Luther continued to be jovial in company, as he declined, some of his worst qualities erupted in his writings. He had always had a tendency to be harsh, to put it mildly, in writing about his opponents, though in his earlier writings, he softened his attacks with self-deprecating wit and apologies for going too far.

But in his last years some of his writings degenerated into sheer invective. He did this in a series of almost obscene tracts against the pope. And he did it against the Jews in a vicious tract entitled *On the Jews and Their Lies* (1543).

This was actually Luther's second treatment of the Jews, and the extent of his decline can be seen by comparing the two books. Back in 1523 Luther wrote *That Jesus Christ Was Born a Jew.* Wanting to bring the gospel to the Jews, he began by answering—in a remarkably, for Luther, nonpolemical way—the objections to Christianity raised by Judaism and gently built the case from the Old Testament that Jesus Christ was the prophesied Messiah. More than that, Luther said that the mistreatment of the Jews by the papacy was what prevented more of them from becoming Christians. He then said that Jews should be given equal rights in society and in commerce. They should be treated with Christ's love.[78]

Elsewhere, Luther lambasted the common rationalization for hating the Jews as Christ killers. Jesus *had* to die if we were to be saved. Jesus *gave Himself* as a sacrifice for our sins. To blame the Jews for killing Him and to kill them in revenge is to miss the whole point of the cross.

But twenty years later, Luther—who had read some sensationalized accounts of what Jews believed about

Jesus—went ballistic, writing that Jews should have their property confiscated, their synagogues destroyed, their writings burned, and be driven out of the country.

The tract is indefensible. True, he advocated expelling the Jews, not killing them. And his hostility was not anti-Semitic in any racial sense; rather, his venom was directed at the Jewish religion. He poured out similar venom against Catholics and enthusiasts, and specifically defended baptized Jews in ways racial anti-Semites never do. Still, the book was used to nourish anti-Semitism in Germany and was used by Adolf Hitler to promote his monstrous program of oppression and genocide.

And yet, as we shall discuss in the final Legacy section of this book, it cannot be more wrong to blame Luther for Hitler. It should be noted that Luther never denied his faults or his sinfulness. In fact, he emphasized them at every opportunity. (He would surely be horrified at the thought that a book might someday be written about him suggesting that people emulate his character.)

For Luther, his sins were real sins. It was for real, not imaginary, sins that Jesus died. Luther understood this, even in his final confusions. A year after the anti-Jewish screed, 1544, he wrote a hymn, "O, You Poor Judas, What Did You Do?":

> 'Twas our great sins and misdeeds gross
> Nailed Jesus, God's true Son, to the cross.
> Thus you, poor Judas, we dare not blame,
> Nor the band of Jews; ours is the shame.[79]

WE ARE BEGGARS

*I*N JANUARY 1546 LUTHER, though he was not feeling well, set off for Eisleben, where he was born and where his relatives still lived, to try to settle a feud between a count and his brother. The controversy involved not just a personal spat but politics, economics, and policies affecting the copper industry, at which Luther's relatives, like his father, still labored.

Luther was sixty-three. Luther's three sons accompanied him. By now Hans was twenty, Martin was fifteen, and Paul was thirteen.

It was cold traveling in winter, and they could not cross the river Saale because of its ice floes and flooding. When he finally got to Eisleben, after eleven days on the road, Luther sent his sons on to Mansfeld to visit their relatives. As the negotiations went on and on, Luther preached in the church for four Sundays and received Holy Communion twice.

Luther had been talking about his death for some time, apparently realizing that the time was near. On February

16 he was heard to say, "If I go back home to Wittenberg, I'll lie down in a coffin and give the maggots a fat doctor to eat."[80] He and Katie wrote frequently back and forth. She was worried about him. In one letter he urged her not to, saying, "I have a caretaker who is better than you and all the angels; he lies in the cradle and rests on a virgin's bosom, and yet, nevertheless, he sits at the right hand of God, the almighty Father. Therefore be at peace."[81]

His last piece of writing was preserved, a short meditation on the possibility of ever sufficiently understanding the Scriptures. The last words he would ever write sum up his view of himself in relation to the abundant, inexhaustible grace of God: "We are beggars, that is true."[82]

Two days later he woke up at 1:00 a.m. with pain and tightness in his chest. His hosts summoned the towns' two physicians along with the count whose problems he had been trying to solve and several of Luther's friends who had been in the city. He was in great pain. He started praying out loud. He thanked God for revealing to him His Son, "whom I have believed, whom I have loved, whom I have preached, confessed, and praised."[83] He started quoting Bible verses: "For God so loved the world that He gave His only begotten Son, that whoever believes in Him should not perish but have everlasting life" (John 3:16). "Our God is the God of salvation; and to GOD the Lord belong escapes from death" (Psalm 68:20). "Lord, now You are letting Your servant depart in peace, According to Your word" (Luke 2:29). Then Psalm 31:5: "Into Your hand I commit my spirit; You have redeemed me, O LORD God of truth," which he repeated three times. Then he was silent.

Luther's friend and fellow Wittenberg theologian Justus Jonas was there, along with the Mansfeld castle preacher, Michael Coelius. They are the ones who later published the eyewitness account of Luther's death. They approached Luther's bed, and one of them shouted loudly, in hopes of being heard, "Reverend father, are you ready to die trusting in your Lord Jesus Christ and to confess the doctrine which you have taught in his name?"

Everyone heard his last word: "Yes!"

PART 2

THE CHARACTER OF MARTIN LUTHER

*Christ must be everything: the beginning, the
middle, and the end of our salvation. We must
lay Him down as the first or foundation stone,
rest the others and intermediate ones on
Him, and also attach the rafters or the roof
to Him. He is the first, the middle, and the last
rung in the ladder to heaven (Genesis 28).
Through Him we must begin, must continue,
and must complete our progress to life.*

—MARTIN LUTHER

A Man of Words

> *The devil does not have the great respect for my*
> *spirit that he has for my speech and pen when*
> *they deal with Scripture.*
>
> —Martin Luther

To think of Luther as a model of leadership, as this series of biographies emphasizes, is somewhat strange, since he exhibited few of the traits normally associated with leadership, at least in the secular self-help section of today's bookstores. He was without ambition and never sought high office or political power. He never set himself up to be a new pope or even a bishop. At his death he was what he remained once he left the monastery: a professor and the city preacher.

He did not have self-esteem or self-confidence. He did not compromise. He did not plan. He was not pragmatic. Actually, he *was* pragmatic once—in giving marriage advice to Philip of Hesse, a wavering prince that he needed on his side—and that was the biggest mistake of his life.

And yet he was indeed a leader, one of the most successful of all time. He blazed a trail all alone, and millions have followed him. Even during his lifetime, princes and commoners asked his advice and deferred to his leadership. Whole principalities did his bidding. A mass movement was launched by his words.

He had no army, no wealth, no institution, no power. All he had was his pulpit and his pen. Luther led sheerly by words. In his case he led by proclaiming the Word of God.

SINNER

*Personally I have nothing good to say for myself;
much less have I anything of which to boast. Like
all human beings, I have been born in sins and
death, under the devil.*

—MARTIN LUTHER

*L*UTHER WOULD PROBABLY RIP his clothes, smear dirt on his face, and launch into one of his scorching polemics if he knew that someone would someday be lifting him up as a role model. Imitate Christ, he would surely say, and then when you realize how miserably you have failed, turn to Him to be your righteousness.

And yet Luther did say it was profitable to study the lives of the saints, not to venerate them nor to imitate their virtues, but rather to imitate their faith, which bore fruit in their virtues. Christianity, Luther kept reminding people in a way that is still needed today, is not about being good. If we were good, we would not need Christ. Christianity is about being forgiven for *not* being good. It is about being *declared* righteous though, if we are honest, we must admit that we are not. It is about being hidden in Christ, who covers our iniquities with His blood, taking upon Himself the punishments we deserve and allowing His righteousness to be imputed as our own.

Luther certainly knew himself as a sinner. His consciousness of his fallen nature—even as he lived an outwardly virtuous life—drove him into the monastery, drove him into Scripture, and drove him to Christ. The joy and liberation he found in the gospel also drove him to oppose the legalistic bureaucracy that Christ's church had been reduced to.

Often people only pay lip service to their imperfections and their sin, actually believing how great they are. Leaders, especially, are prone to this mistake. They are afflicted by egotism, a feeling of superiority to others, and that pride that goeth before the fall. The biggest catastrophes that leaders bring upon themselves and their people are almost invariably due to what the Greeks called *hubris,* the exaltation of the self to the point of acknowledging no limits, whereupon, as the Greeks' tragedies show, the proud man is brought low until he acknowledges his own mortality.

Luther, at least, was spared this pride because he knew he was a sinner utterly dependent on the grace of God.

Saint

*We are all saints, and cursed is he who does not
want to call himself a saint. . . . To call yourself a
saint is, therefore, no presumption but an act of
gratitude and a confession of God's blessings.*
—Martin Luther

*O*NE OF LUTHER'S GREAT spiritual insights is that
a Christian is simultaneously both a saint
and a sinner. We are sinful and we are holy *at the same
time.* This means we are always in a state of inner conflict as we struggle against our sinfulness and as we grow
in the Holy Spirit. Realizing that we are, in fact, saints despite our failures means that we can live and act with the
greatest assurance.

A person becomes a saint by having faith in Jesus
Christ. Not just "faith" by itself. It is the object of faith
that is crucial.

In his Large Catechism, Luther begins his discussion of
the First Commandment ("Thou shalt have no other god
before Me"), by asking first of all what does it mean to
have a god? He concludes that whatever you trust in,
whatever you put your faith in, is your god.

If you have faith in yourself (as is often recommended today), then you are your own god. If you trust in money or the government or science or technology, then that is your god. If you have faith in your family or your profession or progress or that everything will turn out fine, that is your god, just as if you were to put your faith in the Muslims' Allah or in the Hindus' Shiva or the great cosmic oneness.

The only way to avoid idolatry is to put all your trust in the God revealed in His Word, the God who became flesh in Jesus Christ, and to have faith in Him.

"I know no God except the one who became man," he said at Marburg, "and I want no other."[1]

Faith in Christ creates a freedom, a sense of purpose, an assurance the world cannot give.

CALLED

All our work in the field, in the garden, in the city,
in the home, in struggle, in government. . . .
These are the masks of our Lord God, behind
which he wants to be hidden and to do all things.
—MARTIN LUTHER

*L*UTHER DID NOT INTEND to start the Protestant Reformation. He did not intend to start a new church or to break up the old one. He certainly did not intend to dismantle the Middle Ages and to begin the modern world. He believed God was working through him, though a pathetically flawed earthen vessel, to achieve His purposes.

That is, Luther considered that he was carrying out a calling, living out his divinely appointed vocation.

The doctrine of vocation was one of Luther's most profound theological insights, that God gives each Christian particular and unique spheres of service. We live out our faith in our various vocations, a word that simply means "calling." Christians are called to faith by God's Word of the gospel and given vocations in their church, in their particular family, in their work, and in their society. The purpose of every vocation is to love and serve one's neighbors, the human beings God brings into our lives.

Vocation is not just law, however, a responsibility that we must fulfill, though this is part of it. Vocation is also gospel, a function not of our works but of God working through us.

When we pray the Lord's Prayer, Luther pointed out, we ask Him to give us this day our daily bread. He does give us our daily bread. And He does it through the callings of farmers, millers, bakers; we would add truck drivers and factory workers and warehouse attendants and stock boys and the lady at the checkout counter. Soon we have the whole economic system. It is still God who gives us our daily bread, but He has chosen to give us His blessings through human beings.

God creates new life by means of mothers and fathers. He protects us by means of police officers, firefighters, military personnel, judges, and the members of our government. He brings us healing through doctors, nurses, pharmacists, and others with the vocation of health care. He creates beauty through artists. He proclaims His Word and gives us spiritual care through the calling of pastors.[2]

Luther had a strong sense of calling. He knew God was at work through his work. This gave Luther an intense sense of purpose as well as a sense of perspective. His awareness that he was acting not out of his own choices but out of a divinely appointed vocation allowed him both to act with boldness and to relax, trusting all the outcomes to God.

BEARING THE CROSS

> *The cross of Christ is distributed through the*
> *whole world, and to everybody inevitably comes*
> *his portion of it. Do you, therefore, not cast it*
> *aside, but rather take it up as a holy relic, kept not*
> *in a golden or silver case but in a golden heart,*
> *that is, one imbued with gentle love?*
> —MARTIN LUTHER

*L*UTHER ALSO SUFFERED. For all his faith in Christ and the joy he would find in life, Luther would sometimes plunge into deep depression. He was plagued with a succession of physical ailments that often wracked his body with pain. He deeply felt the suffering of others, especially those who were being martyred for the gospel.

Luther also knew failure, or what he thought was failure. He was bitterly frustrated that the established church of the papacy refused to embrace the gospel, that many Christians who said they embraced the gospel did so in hypocrisy, using it as an excuse for immorality. At many times in his career, he wrote that he considered his life and his work of reformation a failure.

But he was no theologian of glory. Luther was a theologian of the cross. His sufferings and his failures forced him to stop depending on himself and to depend more and more on Christ.

Christ's triumph was through the way of the cross—the path of self-denial, what looked like weakness and failure, physical suffering, and spiritual abandonment—and He calls us to take up our cross and follow Him. The difference is that Christ takes up our little crosses into His cross. The suffering Christ meets us in our sufferings, bears us through our trials and tribulations, and grafts us into His own resurrection.[3]

Trusting God's Control

I have committed my cares to our Lord God.
—Martin Luther

*L*UTHER'S FAITH IN CHRIST, which gave him his sense of calling and his ability to deal with setbacks, gave him the conviction that, whatever happened, God was always in control. This, in turn, gave him the ability to let go.

Knowing that God is in control meant that he did not have to fret, scheme, or worry as if the entire outcome of the Reformation were his responsibility. He did not put the burden onto himself; rather, he understood that the burden was carried by Christ. This realization gave Luther great boldness, even recklessness. And yet it also freed him to rest in Christ.

"I did nothing," Luther insisted. "The Word did everything." It was God who was reforming the church and awakening people to the gospel. All Luther did, he would say, was put the Word out; the Word was doing it all.[4]

Likable

> *God wants us to be cheerful, and He hates*
> *sadness. For had He wanted us to be sad, He*
> *would not have given us the sun, the moon, and*
> *the various fruits of the earth. All these He gave*
> *for our good cheer.*
> —Martin Luther

*L*UTHER WAS LIKABLE. By all accounts, even those of his fiercest opponents, he was warm and sociable, enjoyed the pleasures of life, and was pleasant to be around.

He was full of hospitality, and his table was always crowded with friends, visitors, students, and even—in the case of Andreas Karlstadt—a former enemy. The records of those meals in *The Table Talk* show that the dinner conversation consisted of profound theological discourse and also jokes, repartee, and laughter.

Some theologians—as well as some pastors and other leaders—have an air about them of sternness, rectitude, and distance. To be in their presence may be an honor and would surely be edifying, but it would make a person nervous, leery of making a mistake or saying something wrong. That would not be the case with Luther, who—however ferocious he could be in print—was jovial, self-deprecating, and fun to be around in person.

Some leaders are so taken with their sense of authority, their lofty status, and their pride that they lift themselves up over those they are leading, coming across as cold, superior, and unpleasant. Emperor Charles V, who opposed Luther at Worms and Augsburg, was said to have a dour personality and a sour disposition. Someone with great power, of course, can lead that way, intimidating his followers and using force and rewards to keep them in line. But for people to follow voluntarily—of their own free will—and to develop personal bonds of loyalty, they almost always need to like the person they are following, to have affection for the person as well as the cause.

SENSE OF PERSPECTIVE

> *As dear children and heirs of God, we should not*
> *boast of our wisdom, strength, or wealth; we*
> *should boast of the fact that we have the precious*
> *pearl, the dear Word, through which we know*
> *God, our dear Father, and Jesus Christ, whom He*
> *has sent. This is our treasure and heritage; it is*
> *certain and eternal and better than the goods of*
> *all the world.*
>
> —MARTIN LUTHER

*A*GAIN, LUTHER SAW HIMSELF as a small player in
a vast divine plan. This gave him a sense of
perspective. His personal successes and failures—as well
as those of the Reformation—did not matter so much
since God's victory was assured.

This sense of perspective was liberating, allowing him
to act boldly but without self-importance. Another manifestation of Luther's sense of perspective was his teaching
about *adiaphora,* that some things just do not matter. Or
that they do matter as expressions of Christian liberty.

Of course, his sense of perspective also meant that
some things *do* matter. Issues having to do with the Word

of God have an eternal scope, making them far more important than the transient issues that may seem more important at the time, such as the need for military unity to hold off the emperor.

At Marburg he was willing to accept the different ceremonies practiced by the different churches. But he would not compromise his understanding of the Word of God.

PATIENCE

Our Lord God resembles a typesetter, who sets his letters backwards. We definitely see and feel that He is setting His type, but the print we shall see in the beyond. Meanwhile we must have patience.
—MARTIN LUTHER

*L*UTHER'S PERSPECTIVE GAVE HIM patience. He was willing to wait for the Reformation to run its course, understanding that it would take time. He was also patient with people.

When the Reformation was breaking out in Wittenberg, the local congregations were plunged into chaos. Practices ordinary Christians had taken for granted all their lives—such as receiving only the bread in Holy Communion and not the wine—were changed overnight with little preparation or explanation. People found these changes confusing and unsettling, as if everything they had believed and practiced all their lives was now thrown up in the air.

When Luther came out of hiding from the Wartburg, he impressed upon the other Wittenberg reformers the need for patience. People are not ready for some of these changes, he said. Of course the laypeople should receive both the bread and the wine, but they need to be prepared to do so. First comes preaching and teaching the Word of God, he explained, and then the Word will prepare people for the needed changes.

Until the Holy Spirit brings people along, we must be patient with them, taking care not to burden the conscience of those who are still weak in their faith. We should use our Christian liberty to make concessions out of love for the weaker brethren (Romans 14; 1 Corinthians 8).

Patience is born of the conviction that God will act.

Unpragmatic

Why are we so vexed by thoughts, seeing that the future is not in our power for one moment? Let us, then, be satisfied with the present and commit ourselves to the hand of God, who alone knows and controls the past and the future.

—Martin Luther

LUTHER COULD BE VERY impractical. If it were not for Katie, he would have given away all the household money and would have never taken care of himself. And in his leadership of the Reformation, he refused to let political or "real world" considerations trump his convictions.

The pragmatic, common-sense course would have been to compromise with Zwingli on the doctrine of the Lord's Supper so that all the evangelicals and the reformed churches could unite against the common threat. That would have been the politically expedient thing to do.

But, instead, Luther kept pointing to the Bible verse he had written on the table, "THIS IS MY BODY," and was seemingly willing to let the emperor crush the Reformation and burn them all at the stake rather than compromise on the word "is."

Luther refused to be pragmatic when he confessed his faith at Worms, when he left the Wartburg, when he told the elector that he should not resist the emperor's command to turn him over, when he refused the chance to compromise with the pope at Augsburg, and when he set out in bad health in the middle of winter to resolve the noblemen's dispute during the last days of his life.

The one time Luther did decide to go the pragmatic route was when he gave in to Philip of Hesse, who was weak in the faith and wavering in his allegiance but was nevertheless a powerful and important ally. Luther's pragmatism in allowing Philip to commit bigamy made the Reformation a laughingstock in many circles and brought the whole cause into disrepute. That little bit of political pragmatism Luther considered to be the biggest mistake of his life, and he does not seem to have repeated the mistake of being too practical.

Leaders, of course, do have to consider the real world. Luther did too, in his way, as is evident in his patient, flexible approach in the way he dealt with people and in the orderly way he went about reforming the church.

But when leaders try to be overly pragmatic, to the point of sacrificing their convictions in the name of expediency, they often lose their integrity. They often even lose their leadership since they are no longer directing events but rather are being themselves directed by events over which they are exercising no control.

Pragmatism often exalts process over content. To do "whatever works" often sets into motion a course of action in which the overall purpose is forgotten: "Works to do *what?*"

STANDING ALONE

*Christ wants to point out and to warn His
followers that in the world everyone should live as
if he were alone and should consider His Word
and preaching the very greatest thing on earth.*
                                        —MARTIN LUTHER

*W*HEN LUTHER SAID, "HERE I stand," he was
standing alone. This one man was arrayed
against the empire and what presented itself as the church
universal, extending throughout the world and through
the centuries.

Who are you, Von der Eck asked him at Worms, to
question all the scholars and all the theologians and all the
teachers of the Catholic Church? You are just one person.
Are you so much wiser than all of them? Are you the only
one who is right?

Those are powerful questions. What is the difference
between holding on to a personal conviction and having
sinful pride? But Luther knew he was not asserting his
own private opinions or his personal preferences. Of
greater authority than all human beings who have ever

lived is God Himself, and Luther was doing nothing more than standing on His Word.

But how hard it is to stand alone. Peer pressure affects not just children but adults. The ability to go one's own way, despite what everyone else does, is at the essence of leadership.

Many people follow. Those who simply imitate everyone else, follow the trends, and conform to the opinion of the masses are followers by definition. Those who lead have to be willing to act alone.

If they do so only from egotism, though, they are indeed setting themselves up for a fall. True leadership requires being willing to act alone based on a principle or a truth that transcends oneself. And then, perhaps, others will follow.

BOLDNESS

*I*T TOOK BOLDNESS TO defy the pope. To confess his faith before the emperor. To leave the safety of the castle to quell the unrest in Wittenberg.

No one ever doubted Luther's courage. Philip Melanchthon, on the other hand, was not bold. He was a peace-loving, reticent man who tormented himself with worry and second-guessing.

At the Diet of Augsburg, Melanchthon was panicking to the point of seeking a compromise with the pope's theologians. Luther wrote him numerous letters to help keep up his courage. "It is your philosophy which is causing you such trouble," he told him, "not your theology."[5] That is, he was trying to use his formidable reason and his human powers. "God has put this matter into a lesson which is not found in your rhetoric or philosophy; that lesson is *Faith*."

Had Moses tried to comprehend how he might escape the army of Pharoah, Israel would probably be in Egypt to this very day. May God increase your faith and the faith of all of us. If we have that, what can the devil and all the world do to us?[6]

There is another sense of boldness, though, in addition to the courage necessary to face danger and to take up great causes. Boldness can be a stance toward life. Sometimes Melanchthon was paralyzed by guilt and scruples to the point of being unable to act. This is the context of Luther's notorious advice to his friend to "sin boldly." That statement, however, which has been twisted out of context by Luther's opponents, must not be misunderstood. Here is the context, from a letter written in August 1521, eight months after the Diet of Worms:

> If you are a preacher of grace, then preach a true and not a fictitious grace; if grace is true, you must bear a true and not a fictitious sin. God does not save people who are only fictitious sinners. Be a sinner and sin boldly, but believe and rejoice in Christ even more boldly, for he is victorious over sin, death, and the world. . . . Pray boldly—you too are a mighty sinner.[7]

Luther was not saying it is all right to sin. He was not an antinomian—he dealt with them harshly too—but his point is that our sin is real, not just theoretical. We do sin. Sometimes whatever option we choose is going to be tainted by sin. But Christ did not die for "fictitious sin," and He does not offer us a "fictitious grace." Do not be stymied by the fear of committing some sin, as if we have no liberty under the gospel. The key, though, to the passage is the second half of the sentence: if we sin boldly, we are to believe even more boldly. And the more we believe, the more faith we have, and the less we will sin. The point of the passage is not boldness to sin, but the boldness of faith.

Look at all the "boldlys" in the passage: believe boldly, rejoice in Christ boldly, pray boldly.

OPENNESS

We must ever, always, and publicly proclaim the truth or the right doctrine; we are never to slant it or to keep it a secret.

—MARTIN LUTHER

*L*UTHER NEVER SEEMED TO have plotted, conspired, or snuck around in secret. (The one exception that proves the rule is the fiasco of Philip of Hesse's marriages, which were supposed to have been kept secret, but as with most things we want to hide, were soon out in the open.)

Luther even brought his enemies out into the open and publicized the writings that were attacking him. During the controversy over indulgences, Silvester Mazzolini Prierias, a Vatican theologian, wrote a treatise entitled *Dialogue Against the Presumptuous Conclusions of Martin Luther* and sent it to him. Luther's response was to print it! He wanted the public to see how ludicrous were the charges and the arguments against him. (For example, Prierias argued that the authority of the church was *above* that of Scripture.)

Luther then published a rebuttal, maintaining that infallibility belongs only to the Bible. He also cited the testimony of the church fathers and canon law that the church may teach only what is in Scripture.

Prierias wrote a reply. Luther published *that.*

He made this a practice, reprinting and circulating the writings that were against him. He did start adding his own prefaces and notes, pointing out where the criticisms went wrong.

The effect of his openness was to bring the general public into the debates and thus to popularize the Reformation, taking the theological disputes beyond the narrow bounds of academia and the church bureaucracy so that ordinary Christians could see what was at stake.

PRAYER

O God, stand by me in the name of Thy dear Son,
Jesus Christ, who shall be my Protector and
Defender, yea, my mighty Fortress, through the
might and the strengthening of Thy Holy Spirit.
—PRAYER BEFORE THE DIET OF WORMS

*W*HEN HIS GERMAN WRITINGS were collected
and published together in 1539, Luther
wrote an introduction in which he set forth the requirements for the study of theology. He said that becoming a
theologian requires three things: prayer, meditation, and
trial. Those three were keys to Luther's life as a theologian. They are also worth keeping in mind for other
kinds of leadership.

Martin Luther was an athlete of prayer. During his stay
at Coburg during the Diet of Augsburg, a time critical for
the Reformation, Luther prayed. His secretary, Veit Dietrich, witnessed Luther at prayer. He said Luther would
pray at least three hours a day. And those hours were not
in the early morning or late at night, either before or after
the main business of the day. Dietrich said Luther prayed
during the "best hours of the day"; that is, in the middle

of the day, the time of work, when he was at the peak of his energy. [8]

"He alternated between humbly beseeching God and speaking to him in confident faith as one might address a father or friend," said Martin Brecht, summarizing Dietrich's account. "In his prayers he assailed God with his own promises."[9]

"To date," said Luther, "we have for fully fourteen years held back the hostile attack of emperor, Turk, and pope by prayer."[10]

Luther wrote extensively about prayer, especially in his numerous commentaries on the Lord's Prayer. Luther encouraged people to pray the Scriptures, to turn the Psalms and even the Ten Commandments and other texts of the catechism into prayer.

Luther observed that people pray best when they are in greatest need. "There is no better teacher of prayer than need," he wrote.[11] "It is a great thing when a man who feels himself in dire need can turn to prayer. This I know: As often as I have earnestly prayed, prayed in dead earnest, I have certainly been very freely heard and have received more than I had desired."[12]

MEDITATION

*Nothing more beautiful in the eyes of God than a
soul that loves to hear His Word.*

—MARTIN LUTHER

S OMEONE WHO WISHES TO be a theologian, Luther
said, must not only pray but meditate. By meditation, Luther meant the study and the contemplation of
Scripture. We should let him explain from his 1539 preface to his German works:

> You should meditate. This means that not only in your
> heart but also externally you should constantly handle
> and compare, read and reread the Word as preached and
> the very words as written in Scripture, diligently noting
> and meditating on what the Holy Spirit means. Moreover,
> be careful that you do not become surfeited and get the
> notion that, having read, heard, and repeated it once or
> twice, you have done enough and understand everything
> completely. . . . For God wants to give you His Spirit only
> through the external Word.[13]

Luther's own practice was to read the Bible through
twice every year.[14] In addition, he used the Scriptures in his

personal devotions and with his children. He described his practice in a sermon just prior to the Diet of Augsburg:

> You should diligently learn the Word of God and by no means imagine that you know it. Let him who is able to read take a psalm in the morning, or some other chapter of Scripture, and study it for a while. This is what I do. When I get up in the morning, I pray and recite the Ten Commandments, the Creed, and the Lord's Prayer with the children, adding any one of the psalms.[15]

To read the Bible effectively, he said, you will look for Christ in its pages.

TRIAL

> *This work of God goes on till death. Through this work Christendom became so great and strong. Through it the beloved martyrs went to heaven. Through it the holy Fathers were enlightened in the Scriptures. Through it Christians become experienced and trained people, good for giving advice and help in all things.*
>
> —MARTIN LUTHER

A THEOLOGIAN, SAID LUTHER, is made by prayer, meditation on Scripture, and finally, trial. The Latin word he used was *tentatio.* That word's meaning embraces the senses of "trial" but also "attack," "assault," and "temptation."

Luther must have had in mind his own spiritual struggles with which he was afflicted at various points throughout his life. He described them as assaults of the devil, as conflicts between his sinful nature and Christ. They involved a mood of depression that was little short of despair.

"I have passed through unspeakable trials—trials in which no creature was able to counsel me," he confessed. "I have passed through trials of such a nature that I thought no one on earth had them before."

There would never have been any remedy and advice for difficulties so great, for temptations so grievous, if Christ had not come to open the Bible to me and to advise and comfort me with His Word. Thus God (as Paul says, 2 Cor. 1:3–4) comforts us in all our tribulations so that we are able to comfort those who are in affliction.[16]

Luther believed that going through such negative experiences is *helpful* in the formation of a theologian, and by extension, a pastor or other leader. Mere book learning is not enough. But mere experience is not enough, either. Luther stresses the role of *painful* experience.

Has the person who wants us to trust his spiritual advice and wants us to follow him ever gone through *trials?* Has this person's alleged wisdom survived testing?

We are so used to judging people—and ourselves—in terms of "success," that we sometimes forget the importance of suffering in shaping character. In Luther's terms, our attention to victories, prosperity, and pragmatic results is part of our "theology of glory," as opposed to the much more fruitful and realistic "theology of the cross."

Having survived trials and tribulations and personal struggles gives credibility to a person who presumes to teach about spiritual matters. Those who have gone through periods of difficulties, doubt, and temptation will tend to have more empathy and understanding with the struggles of other people. Battle-tested "theologians" can thus be more effective in evangelizing, counseling, and teaching those in need of their ministry.

Ignoring Self-Interest

Man can seek only his own interests and love himself above all things.

—Martin Luther

*L*UTHER SHOWED A CURIOUS indifference to his own self-interest. Despite his prominence and influence, though princes and nations sought his counsel, Luther refused to seek any kind of power or position. He was never more than a small-town preacher and university professor.

Nor did he seek wealth. Luther refused to take money for any of his writings. They contributed to the prosperity of the new printing industry, but Luther did not profit from his writings, not even his translation of the Bible.

Luther often urged the princes to act directly against his own interests. If the emperor commands you to turn me over to him, he kept telling the elector, you must obey. You princes and members of the Smalcald League, you should not take arms against the emperor if he chooses to put down the Reformation by force.

Most leaders act to advance their self-interest or that of the people they are leading. And yet, being able to set aside one's own interests can free a leader to act on principle.

HATING CHAOS

Now it is better to suffer wrong from one tyrant,
that is, from the ruler, than from unnumbered
tyrants, that is, from the mob.
                                                    —MARTIN LUTHER

*L*UTHER HATED CHAOS. He truly believed in the
importance of order—in the life of an individual, in the church, and in society.

When the church at Wittenberg degenerated into riots,
vandalism, disorder, and fanaticism, Luther left the safety
of the Wartburg to bring order to the Reformation.

When the peasants, exhilarated by their new spiritual
freedom, rose up in a revolution that amounted to anarchy, Luther urged the earthly rulers to restore social order
at any cost.

Luther resolutely opposed the enthusiasts, whose trust
was in their emotions and in the god within rather than in
the objective Word of God. He opposed the elimination of
all order in worship services. He distrusted subjectivism,
individualistic theology, and radical extremism, whether
in the church or the state.

Most leaders hate to see things spinning out of control.
The danger of chaos is why we need leaders.

ANGER

*You must not get angry with anyone, regardless of
the injury he may have done to you. But where
your office requires it, there you must get angry,
even though no injury has been done to you.*
—MARTIN LUTHER

*L*UTHER HAD HIS BAD qualities, of course, and
one of them was an unbridled anger that
would sometimes break out in his polemical writings.
Even many of the people on his side felt that the tone of
his polemics sometimes made them less effective than
they should have been.

Luther preached against the vice of anger, and he acknowledged his own guilt. And yet there is an anger that is
not a sin. It is possible to be angry but not sin (Ephesians
4:26). Luther said there could even be an "anger of love":

Anger is indeed necessary sometimes, but only in those
whose responsibility it is, and only if one does not go beyond the punishment of sin and evil. . . . In other words,
it is an anger of love, one that wishes nobody any evil,
one that is friendly to the person but hostile to the sin.[17]

Luther went so far as to say that anger can be spiritually helpful. "In grave temptations," he once said, "two responses are good: (1) steadfast faith in Christ, (2) fierce and strong anger."[18] A person being tempted needs to get angry at the sin, whereupon it will lose its attraction.

And in an observation that might apply to other leaders, Luther found that in his own life, anger actually increased his effectiveness. "I have found no better remedy than anger," he was recorded to have said in *The Table Talk*. "If I want to write, pray, preach well, then I must be angry. Then my entire blood supply refreshes itself, my mind is made keen, and all temptations depart."[19]

GENEROUS

*[We] ought freely to help our neighbor through
our body and its works, and each one should
become as it were a Christ to the other that we
may be Christs to one another.*
—MARTIN LUTHER

*L*UTHER WAS EXTREMELY GENEROUS. He accepted
no money for his writings. Nor did he charge
his students for his lectures. Nor did he charge the students who lived with him for their room and board. The
elector offered him a silver mine as payment for his translation of the Bible, but Luther turned it down.

Luther was always giving money to refugees fleeing persecution, to impoverished university students, to homeless
people. He was also always inviting people to stay in his
home and to eat at his table.

The Luthers had six children. In addition, they took in
four orphaned children from among their relatives. Also,
Katie's aunt, Magdalena, or "Aunt Lene," lived with them
and helped with the children. The Luthers also offered
their large house, the former monastery, as a hospital, taking in the sick, particularly when Wittenberg was afflicted
with the plague. Then there were the students who lived

with them. At one point, there were twenty-five people in the Luther household.[20]

It was up to Katie to bring order to the family's finances. Sometimes she and her husband clashed over money. She insisted that the boarders pay their way. She managed every penny. She earned extra income from her garden, the orchard, and her livestock. Luther did appreciate the way she kept them solvent.

Katie tried to keep Luther's generosity under some control, but to little avail. Once a student needed money and asked Luther for help. But there was no money in the house. So Luther picked up a silver cup, which had been a wedding present. Katie apparently shot him a look. Luther crumpled up the cup, telling the student, "This cup no longer serves any useful purpose; take it to the goldsmith and keep the money he gives you for it."[21]

The most dramatic example of Luther's generosity—and Katie's long-suffering support—was on their wedding night. The guests had just left, at 11:00 p.m., when there was a knock on the door. It was Andreas Karlstadt, Luther's nemesis, fleeing the Peasants' War. He had to sneak into town at night to avoid the magistrate.[22]

Here was the man who tried to hijack the Reformation while Luther was in the Wartburg. Karlstadt brought anarchy into the church. And then, when he was driven out of Wittenberg, he brought anarchy into the state, agitating for the peasants to revolt, which led to their slaughter. Now he was on the run. He went to the man he had opposed and attacked and refuted. He threw himself on Luther's mercy. On Luther's wedding night, no less. And Luther and Katie took him in.

A Man of the People

> *A Christian is a perfectly free lord of all, subject to none. A Christian is a perfectly dutiful servant of all, subject to all.*
>
> —Martin Luther

*L*UTHER ACCEPTED THE EXISTING social order for the most part, and the late Middle Ages were characterized by rigid social hierarchies. So it is especially remarkable how egalitarian Luther was. That is, he accepted all people, from all ranks of life, as equally valuable.

Amid all the vast political and diplomatic and theological issues he had to deal with, his main priority was his pulpit, where he preached to everyday people from all walks of life in a way that connected with them all.

Princes and lords clamored to consult with Luther, and he would help them if he could, but he was just as willing to spend time with ordinary folks, helping them in their spiritual needs.

For example, Luther once wrote a book for his barber. While cutting Luther's hair, Peter the barber would ask him all kinds of questions about how he should pray. So in 1535 Luther wrote *A Simple Way to Pray: For a Good*

Friend. It was dedicated to Master Peter and was widely circulated among ordinary Christians who profited greatly from the practical, down-to-earth advice about how to pray with Scripture and how to pray from the heart.

> A good, active barber must keep his thoughts, mind, and eyes closely on the razor and the hair and must not forget where he is with his stroke and shave. But if he wants to gossip freely at the same time or let his thoughts or eyes go elsewhere, he may well cut off a man's mouth and nose and his throat besides. Thus every matter, if it is to be done well, calls for the attention of the whole person, with all his senses and members. . . . How much more does prayer, if it is to be a good prayer, require a heart that is undistracted, entirely and solely given to its devotion![23]

REMEMBERING HIS
OTHER CALLINGS

God lays souls into the lap of married people,
souls begotten from their own body, on which
they may practice all Christian works. For when
they teach their children the Gospel, parents are
certainly their apostles, bishops, and ministers.
—MARTIN LUTHER

ONE REASON LUTHER HONORED his barber and
people like him was that he understood the
doctrine of vocation. All callings, no matter how humble in
the world's eyes, are the gifts of God to His people. All are
avenues of service to one's neighbor and ways of glorifying
God through one's work.

Luther knew that our vocations are multiple, that we
have a calling not only in the work that God has given us
to do—whether launching a Reformation or cutting hair,
all vocations being equal before God—but also in our citi-
zenship and in our families.

This is something that many leaders forget. They throw
themselves into their work or their mission but neglect
their families.

Luther himself was extraordinarily busy, as we have seen. He poured his energy into his primary calling as the preacher of the city church. In his related calling as a doctor of the church, a professor of the university theology faculty, he studied, he wrote out his lectures, and he taught. As the man God called to reform the church from its abuses and to turn it back to the Word of God, Luther wrote tirelessly and fearlessly.

Yet he did not forget his callings as a husband and a father. We have seen the affection between Martin and Katie. He also displayed his love for his children.

In his writings he often stressed the need for parents to be gentle with their children, to discipline them, yes, but then to make up with them. "One should punish children and pupils in such a way that the apple always lies beside the rod; for it is bad if children and pupils lose their friendly disposition towards parents and teachers."[24] This was not just the rather advanced notion for his time that children be governed with rewards as well as punishments. After parents use the rod, he was suggesting, they should give the child an apple as part of restoring the relationship.

"A father should handle his children in the manner in which we observe God handling us," he wrote. The law is followed by the gospel.

> In the midst of the affliction He consoles, strengthens, confirms, nourishes, and favors us. . . . Moreover, when we have repented, He instantly remits the sins as well as the punishments. In the same manner parents ought to handle their children.[25]

Even when Luther was engaged in the great, historic work of the Reformation, he was thinking about his wife and children, writing them heartfelt letters and keeping them in his prayers. While he was at Coburg during the critical deliberations of the Diet of Augsburg, Luther took the time to write a letter to four-year-old Hans, whom he addressed with the diminutive "Hänschen." In the letter, he spun out a fanciful story, filled with the toys and pastimes he knew his little boy loved. In doing so, he gave his child a glimpse, in terms the four-year-old could relate to, of what heaven would be like for him:

> I know a nice, beautiful garden with many children in golden dresses, gathering beautiful apples under the trees, as well as plums, cherries, mirabelles, and pears. They sing, jump, and are happy. They also have beautiful ponies with bridles of gold and silver saddles. I asked the owner of the garden, "Whose are these children?" And he answered, "These are the children who like to say their prayers, read, and are devout." Then I said, "Dear sir, I also have a son, his name is Hänschen Luther, could he not also come into this garden, eat the delicious apples and pears, ride the beautiful ponies, and play with these children?" Then the man replied, "If he also likes to say his prayers, learn, and is devout, then, by all means he, too, may come into the garden."
>
> And he showed me there in the garden a beautiful meadow, prepared for dancing, with golden flutes, drums and silver crossbows. But it was still early and the children had not yet eaten their breakfast, that's why I couldn't wait for the dance. So I told the man, "Dear sir, I will go

right away and write all this to my son Hänschen, that he will study hard, pray well, and be devout so he, too, may come into this garden. But he also has a Muhme Lene [Katie's aunt]; he must bring her too." Then the man said, "That's fine, go ahead and write him accordingly."[26]

Accepting Paradox

*In order that there may be room for faith, it is
necessary that all that is believed be hidden; but
these matters cannot be hidden more deeply than
when they, as it appears to us, are the very
opposite of what we feel and experience.*
—Martin Luther

A CHARACTERISTIC OF LUTHER as a theologian
and as a thinker is his grasp of paradox.
Some things seem like contradictions, but they are simply
two poles of truth.

Christianity itself hinges on paradoxes. Jesus Christ is
both God *and* man. Human beings are fallen, depraved
sinners *and* the gifted, valuable images of God. We are
saved by the death *and* the resurrection of Jesus Christ.

Luther sharpened our understanding of the gospel with
paradoxes of his own. Christians are *both* saints *and* sinners. We are lords of all things *and* we are servants of all.
We are under the law *and* the gospel.

What is distinctive to Luther's theology are more paradoxes. He wrote both *Bondage of the Will* and *The Freedom of the Christian.* The Lord's Supper is ordinary bread and wine *and* it is the body and blood of Christ.

This way of thinking—embracing apparent contradictions as parts of a larger truth—makes possible a broadness of mind that can take in whatever it faces without losing its bearings.

FIGHTING THE DEVIL

*All the cunning of the devil is exercised in trying
to tear us away from the Word.*

—MARTIN LUTHER

CHRISTIANS TODAY OFTEN FORGET about the devil. To Luther, Satan was real and a constant adversary. The devil was in the corruptions of the papacy, in the machinations of the political scene, in his trials and depressions.

Luther distinguished between the "black devil," who tempts us with overt evil and afflicts us with trials, and the "white devil," who is disguised as an angel of light and who seeks to destroy us by means of good-seeming heresies and false righteousness.

Luther also describes literal demonic assaults. In the Wartburg, while he was translating the Bible, Luther made it sound like the set of *The Exorcist.* Luther reported mysterious, poltergeist-like noises in the castle, like a hundred barrels rolling down the stairs. Once the devil appeared to him as a big black dog lying on his bed. Luther said he threw it out the window, and it disappeared.[27]

Luther may well have thrown ink at the devil while he was in the Wartburg, but the reference may be to his writing that he was throwing at the devil. Surely Luther's translation of the Bible was a monumental blow against Satan. If anything would provoke the devil to direct action, it would be someone on the verge of releasing the Word of God into the world.

Luther said the devil would sometimes speak to him in the night, disputing over his soul, trying to torment him with doubts, making him tremble and sweat. Luther told of a time when the devil told him that he was a great sinner. "I knew that long ago," Luther replied. "Tell me something new. Christ has taken my sins upon himself, and forgiven them long ago. Now grind your teeth."[28]

When the devil accuses you of your sins, Luther said in a sermon, that should put a great sword and weapon into your hands, because it should remind you of Christ. "To Him I direct you," is what we should say to the devil. "You may accuse and condemn Him. Let me rest in peace; for on His shoulders, not on mine, lie all my sins and the sins of all the world."[29]

The devil can be defeated, he said, with texts of Scripture and by confessing Christ. Give him not a long speech but a brief reply, such as, "I am a Christian, of the same flesh and blood as is my Lord Christ, the Son of God. Settle your account with Him."[30] Ultimately, the devil is nothing more than a chained dog that can only frighten but not harm a Christian. So the best way to handle the devil is to jeer and mock him.

HUMOR

You have as much laughter as you have faith.
———MARTIN LUTHER

"THAT PROUD SPIRIT CANNOT stand to be scorned,"
Luther noted.[31] His practice of using humor
against Satan might be similar to his practice of throwing
ink at him. He may have thrown jokes and ink at literal
manifestations of the devil. But more important, he used
both ink and humor against the devil in his writings.

Luther is one of the relatively few theologians who, in
the midst of some profound spiritual discussion, could
make readers laugh.

Luther's polemical writings against his opponents em-
ploy satire, sarcasm, lampoons, and insults. Some people
are put off by Luther's rapier tongue. But these shots at enemies, many of whom are now long forgotten, are often
laugh-at-loud funny.

Luther's detractors called him rude and crude. They
were shocked by his occasionally vulgar language with all
kinds of embarrassing references to "bodily functions."
What needs to be remembered, as those who read old
books know, is that virtually everyone before the Victorian
Age of the nineteenth century was relatively coarse by

post-Victorian standards. People five hundred years ago lived in an earthier, less sanitary time. The distinguished biographer Roland Bainton said the actual amount of vulgarity in Luther's writing is small and no worse than many of his contemporaries.[32] "Luther delighted less in muck than many of the literary men of his age," Bainton commented, "but if he did indulge, he excelled in this as in every other area of speech."[33]

He had a gentler sense of humor, too. His sermons and commentaries are full of witty observations, amusing anecdotes, and comical ways of putting things.

Not that Luther told jokes in the modern way as a means of getting people's attention or keeping an audience entertained. His humor was part of his sensibility and a natural part of his thinking and expressing.

IMMOVABLE

*Merciful God! Thou hast made it possible for me
to become a Christian; help me to stay a Christian
and to increase in faith from day to day. Even if
the entire world fell away, and everybody joined
the sects, and the devil broke all vessels, I would
pay no attention to it, but with Thy divine help I
would abide by the Gospel.*

—MARTIN LUTHER

*L*UTHER WAS STUBBORN. That can be a fault. He
seldom backed down. And yet that can also
be a virtue.

Arguing against indulgences, standing before the emperor and his diet, disputing with Zwingli at Marburg—
Luther took nothing back, nor would he change his
course. This refusal to compromise created problems for
the princes and split the Reformation.

Sometimes the way to deal with a personal weakness is
to channel it in an unselfish way in the service of a greater
cause. Luther sought to deny himself and his own interests and pride. Luther did, in fact, take back some of his

own opinions, saying that in the early days of the indulgence controversy he was too positive toward the pope!

When Luther was being immovable, at least in his mind, it was not about *his* opinion but about the necessity to stand on the Word of God. It is the Word of God that does not move.

CHRISTIAN LIBERTY

*This liberty is a spiritual liberty. It does not suspend
the Law; but it supplies what the Law demands,
that is, love and delight. Accordingly, the Law is
quieted and need no longer drive and demand.*
—MARTIN LUTHER

*T*HE LIFE OF THE Christian flows out of the
gospel. Christ frees our wills from the
bondage of sin, and living faith bears fruit in good works.
All of this grows out of Christian liberty.

Luther rejected every kind of legalism—whether from
the pope or the enthusiasts—that bases our relationship to
God on what we have to do, as opposed to what God has
done for us. He rejected as tyranny any attempts to re-
strict Christian liberty, to burden people's consciences,
and to impose man-made rules and restrictions. Here is
what he told the Church of Rome (from *The Babylonian
Captivity of the Church* [1520]):

Neither pope nor bishop nor any man has the right to impose a single syllable of law upon a person who is a Christian unless it is done with his consent. Whatever is done

otherwise, is done in the spirit of tyranny. . . . Only on behalf of this liberty of conscience I raise my voice and con-
fidently cry: Upon Christians no laws may be imposed by
any right, neither by men nor by angels, without their
consent; for we are free from all things.[34]

Here is what he told the enthusiasts, who insisted that
Christians had to follow a new set of spiritual rules (from
Against the Heavenly Prophets [1525]):

Friend, do not consider it a trifle to forbid what God does
not forbid, to destroy the Christian liberty that cost Christ
his blood, to burden consciences with sin where there is
no sin. He who has the audacity to do this will also be au-
dacious enough to commit any wrong; yea, he has
thereby already renounced all that God is, teaches, and
does, including His Christ.[35]

Christian freedom is a spiritual reality. We still have
physical restrictions. We remain subject to laws and governments. Tyrants may still oppress us. But they cannot
take away our freedom in Christ.

In a 1532 sermon Luther graphically described what
he may well have faced himself at the hands of the pope
and the emperor, as well as the grounds of his defiance:

If I am actually flung into prison and the pope binds me
with ropes, I am nonetheless arrogant and defiant and say
to him: You, pope, are my servant, and I am the lord of
these chains or of this prison; for they shall not take this
liberty from me, and they shall be no hindrance to my

faith and Christianity. These bonds shall not harm me;
rather they shall be useful to me and bring me closer to
Christ; and the more you torture and plague me with
prison, with laws, temptations, and fears, the better you
are serving me.[36]

TRUSTS SCRIPTURE

*People think: If I could hear God speaking in His
own Person, I would run so fast to hear Him that
my feet would bleed. . . . But now you have the
Word of God in church, in books, in your home;
and this is as certainly God's Word as if God
Himself were speaking.*

—MARTIN LUTHER

*T*HE WORD OF GOD, to Luther, was literally God's
voice by which He created the world and con-
tinues to reveal Himself to human beings. The Word of
God became flesh in Jesus Christ (John 1:1–14). God's
Word is living and active, accomplishing His purposes and
cutting through to the human heart (Hebrews 4:12). God's
Word of law brings conviction of sin, and God's Word of
gospel engenders faith. The Holy Spirit, Luther believed, is
at work in God's Word.

God has committed His Word to human beings who
can express that Word in human language. God's Word is
embodied concretely and authoritatively in the Bible. But
God's Word can also be proclaimed in a sermon or in a
conversation that says how Christ died for sinners.

According to the Church of Rome, the church existed before the Word. It was the church, the Catholic theologians taught, that selected the books that would make up the canon of the Bible. Therefore, the church is the judge of the Word.

Not so, said Luther. The Word existed before the church. How could anyone have heard of Christ, so they could join the church, unless they had been told about Him through human language? God's Word, Luther believed, was living and active in that message. "It is not the Word of God because the church says so," he said, "but that the Word of God might be spoken, therefore the church comes into being. The church does not make the Word, but it is made by the Word."[37]

Now God's Word is to be found in its fullness in the pages of the Bible. Some liberal theologians today are saying that the doctrine of the inerrancy of Scripture is recent in the history of the church, a creation of eighteenth- or nineteenth-century theologians. But Luther clearly taught the inerrancy of Scripture. He said so in the Large Catechism: "My neighbor and I—in short, all men—may err and deceive, but God's Word cannot err."[38]

Some of Luther's critics point to places in his writings in which he questioned whether certain books really belong in the canon of the Bible. The epistle of James, for example, which seems to say that we are justified by works instead of by faith (James 2:24), which would contradict other passages that say we are justified by faith apart from works (Romans 3:28). Of course, as Luther himself came to see, the passages do not contradict each other, since James is speaking of a "living" faith that bears fruit in good

works as opposed to a "dead" faith. Luther also was not a
fan of the book of Revelation, since he could not figure
out what it was supposed to mean, complaining that a
"revelation" should "reveal."

The issue of what books belong in the canon was one
the Reformation had to come to terms with once the Reformers restored the Bible to its central place. For example, the Apocrypha—those books in Greek that come
between the Old Testament and the New Testament—are
considered authoritative in the Roman Catholic Church,
but Protestants, for many reasons, reject their divine authority. But that Luther at one time raised questions about
some of the books does not mean that he did not ultimately accept them. Nor does it mean that he did not
have an extremely high view of Scripture, which in fact
was one of his most important theological legacies.

The bottom line for Luther was that the Bible is true.
Furthermore, it is clear. We must follow God's revelation
in Scripture and not our human reason nor our human
emotions. "My dear pope, you must not lord it over Scripture, nor must I or anybody else, according to our own
ideas," Luther once said in a sermon. "We should rather
allow Scripture to rule and master us, and we ourselves
should not be the masters, according to our own mad
heads, setting ourselves above Scripture."[39]

CLINGS TO CHRIST

Do not flutter around with your thoughts, do not climb up to God by another way than through Jesus Christ. For Christ is the Bridge and the Way, and you should say: I will teach no Christian anything higher and further than the Lord Christ, born of Mary; for I am not to construct a way of my own to God by my thoughts.

—MARTIN LUTHER

*C*HRISTOLOGY IS AT THE heart of Luther's theology—his understanding of God, salvation, the sacraments, the Christian life—and it is also at the heart of his devotional life.

God has become man for our salvation, and we must "cling to Christ" in all of our trials, sufferings, doubts, and joys. The risen and ascended Christ is truly present in His Word and in the sacraments. "I am with you always," He promised, "to the end of the age" (Matthew 28:20).

Christ bears our sins, endures our punishment, and grants us His own righteousness. He does *everything* for us. So for us,

Christ must be everything: the beginning, the middle, and the end of our salvation. We must lay Him down as the first or foundation stone, rest the others and intermediate ones on Him, and also attach the rafters or the roof to Him. He is the first, the middle, and the last rung in the ladder to heaven (Genesis 28). Through Him we must begin, must continue, and must complete our progress to life.[40]

DIES IN FAITH

In Baptism all Christians begin to die, and
continue to die until they reach their graves.
—MARTIN LUTHER

*L*uther knew that death was not easy. "I do
not see people glad to die," he once told Veit
Dietrich. "I prefer to see them fear and tremble and turn
pale before death but nevertheless pass through it. Great
saints do not like to die. The fear of death is a penalty;
therefore it is something sad."[41] He noted that animals die
easier, but human beings instinctively know that they
must face God's judgment.[42] And yet "to know how to die
is reserved for the Christians."[43]

> When temptation assails you on your deathbed and your
> spirit becomes oppressed and does not know which way
> to turn, you should above all things center your attention
> on the external Word and cling to it; otherwise there is
> no help.[44]

> When I am to die, I must boldly rely on Christ, submit
> my head to the stroke of death, and boldly trust the Word
> of God. This cannot deceive me. In that hour faith must

go straight ahead, nor allow itself to be led astray by anything; it must banish all that it sees, hears, and feels.[45]

In these quotations, much of what Luther wrote
throughout his life came together: Clinging to Christ.
Trusting the Word of God that is "external" to one's own
thoughts and feelings. And doing all of this "boldly."

This describes how Luther died. He endured his final
trial, his final struggle, when he was in the throes of death.
As his body was wracked with pain, he called out verses of
Scripture. He called on Christ. With his last breath, he confessed his faith.

PART 3

THE LEGACY OF MARTIN LUTHER

*Martin Luther, German theologian and religious
reformer, initiated the Protestant Reformation,
and his vast influence, extending beyond religion
to politics, economics, education, and language,
has made him one of the crucial figures in
modern European history.*

—DESCRIPTION OF LUTHER ON THE
ISLAND OF FREEDOM WEBSITE

WHAT HAPPENED NEXT

*L*UTHER DIED ON FEBRUARY 18, 1546. Five months later, on July 15, the emperor attacked. The Smalcald League mustered its armies. Duke Moritz, though a nominal evangelical who ruled the regions of Saxony not governed by the elector, betrayed the league and joined with the emperor in return for grants of land and privileges. In the battle of Mühlberg, on April 24, 1547, the army of the Smalcald League was totally defeated.

The emperor imprisoned Elector John Frederick and Philip of Hesse. In May the emperor occupied Wittenberg. He went to the church where Luther was buried and stood at his tomb. His men urged him to dig up Luther's body, burn it, and scatter the ashes. The emperor replied, "I do not make war against dead men."[1]

Emperor Charles V proceeded to restore Catholicism in the evangelical lands. He allowed the priests to stay married and for the laity to receive the cup in Holy

Communion until the conclusion of the long-awaited church council, which finally convened at Trent in December 1545. Otherwise, the Church of Rome was brought back to power.

But then Duke Moritz, who had been given the elector's domain and now ruled all of Saxony, grew angry with the emperor, who had not given him all the land he had been promised. Moritz conspired with the king of France. Having betrayed the Smalcald League, he now betrayed the emperor. In the spring of 1552 Duke Moritz staged a surprise attack on the emperor at Innsbruck and defeated his army. The emperor fled for his life.

Elector John Frederick and Philip of Hesse were freed. Duke Moritz won another victory but was killed in battle. The emperor, defeated and worn out from the decades of religious conflict, finally gave up. The Peace of Augsburg, ratified on September 25, 1555, formally recognized the right of Protestants to exist.

The word *protestant* was a term used to refer to the princes who had formally "protested" the Edict of Worms back in 1529.[2] The Peace of Augsburg, however, recognized only those who accepted the Augsburg Confession, not Zwinglians, Calvinists, or Anabaptists. Religious freedom was given only to the princes, so that the religion of the ruler determined the religion of the country. Those who could not accept the religion of their prince were free to emigrate to another country where their religion was practiced. Catholics were to be tolerated in the imperial cities, even those that were ruled by evangelicals. The Imperial Supreme Court was to have representatives from both the Catholics and the evangelicals.[3] The Peace of

Augsburg did not provide complete religious liberty. But it was a huge step in that direction.

The Peace of Augsburg lasted for more than half a century, until the conflict between Catholicism and Protestantism broke out again in the Thirty Years' War (1618–48), a terrible European-wide conflict that destroyed medieval society forever. On its rubble was built the modern world. And Luther started it all.

Whatever Happened to Them?

*A*FTER LUTHER DIED, KATIE was grief stricken. When the emperor marched on Wittenberg, young Hans Luther reportedly manned the walls in its defense. Katie loaded up a wagon with the family's possessions and fled to Magdeburg. When she came back, she found that troops had destroyed her crops, chopped down her fruit trees, and killed her livestock. She started over, taking in students as boarders once again. She died seven years later. She showed that she shared her husband's faith and his way with words. On her deathbed she said that she would "cling to Christ like a burr on a dress."[4]

Their children grew up, got married, and they and their descendants became ordinary people.

Philip Melanchthon, his old friend and spine-stiffener gone, became a compromiser. Duke Moritz had asked him to draw up some articles that the evangelical princes could follow to keep the gospel alive during the Catholic occupation. The result was the Augsburg Interim, which asserted justification by faith but said that the Catholic ceremonies could be tolerated as *adiaphora*. After the

Peace of Augsburg, Melanchthon made overtures to the Calvinists, formulating an explanation of the Lord's Supper that, by its vagueness, could be acceptable to both parties. But then he developed the notion that salvation involves the cooperation of the believer's will and God's will. This "synergism" would be closer to the Arminianism that would come later than to either Calvin and Luther, both of whom were "monergists," believing that salvation is the work of God alone.

Melanchthon went so far as to publish a revised Augsburg Confession to reflect his own views—after all, he must have thought, he wrote it, so he should be able to revise it—and his new version of Lutheranism attracted followers. He died in 1560 and was buried next to Luther. But a new generation of young Lutheran theologians emerged—James Andreae, David Chytraeus, Martin Chemnitz—who forged the Formula of Concord, which, collected together with the other Lutheran confessions in the Book of Concord in 1580, ensured that Lutheranism would remain both sacramental and monergistic, following the theology of Martin Luther.

Ulrich Zwingli's followers split just before he was killed in a battle with Swiss Catholics. Zwingli believed in infant baptism, but some of his followers did not. These, joining with the Anabaptist survivors of the Peasants' War, started another theological tradition. Some of those survivors—those who believed in peace rather than violent revolution—started Mennonite and Amish communities. The more mainstream Baptists would thrive in England. Enthusiasts would periodically emerge in England, the Netherlands, and elsewhere. In the meantime, the Reformed tradition begun by Zwingli in Switzerland would find its greatest theologian in John Calvin, whose influence soon spread to both the Anglicans and the Puritans in England, and from there to America, where Lutheran settlers from Germany and Scandinavia also were making their homes.

All of these different varieties of Protestantism, when they spoke German—including the Amish, to this day—read Luther's translation of the Bible.

As for Luther's great adversary, the pope, the great church council that many of the Reformers put their hope in was finally held at Trent, in northern Italy. Though it was supposed to be an "ecumenical council," of course the evangelicals were not invited. The Council of Trent did finally deal with the financial and moral corruption that had made the medieval church lose so much credibility. But it reasserted in even stronger terms the teachings that had sparked the Reformation. The Council of Trent pronounced a solemn curse on anyone who believed in the doctrine of justification by faith, along with other Reformation doctrines, declaring those teachings "anathema."

The Council of Trent launched the "Counter-Reformation" designed to instill a distinctive Roman Catholic piety as a way to dampen the appeal of the Reformation gospel. The bishops at Trent acknowledged that the lack of education among the people was a problem, so they started teaching orders and founded schools. And when the new teaching orders searched for a curriculum for the new Catholic schools, they adapted the curriculum developed by Melanchthon and Luther.

HIS LEGACY FOR THE CHURCH

*T*HE ENGLISH EDITION OF Luther's works con
tains fifty-five volumes. That is an enormous
amount of writing. But it represents less than half of
Luther's total output.[5]

Luther's writings in German and Latin fill 127 large
volumes. That compilation of Luther's complete works, a
German project known as the Weimar edition, was begun
in 1883 and completed in 2002. The edition contains
some 75,000 pages.

Luther's greatest theological work is not his polemical
writings, which figure more in discussions of his biography, but his Bible commentaries. These were mostly
based on the lectures he had given on the different books
of the Bible as a university professor, which he did, day in
and day out, throughout all the controversies, for most of
his life. He published commentaries on much of the Bible.
Of particular note are his commentaries on Genesis, Isa-
iah, the minor prophets, and the Psalms. But his most famous and influential are his commentaries on Romans
and Galatians.

Luther's commentaries on Romans and Galatians are practically unrivaled in their insight and evangelical power. John Bunyan, the Puritan author of *Pilgrim's Progress,* said that in the Galatians commentary he found the book that was "most fit for a wounded conscience." He said, "I do prefer this book of Martin Luther upon the Galatians (excepting the Holy Bible) before all the books that ever I have seen."[6]

John Wesley, the English evangelist who began a theological tradition of his own, attended a meeting of Moravians (Lutheran pietists) at Aldersgate on May 24, 1738. They were reading out loud Luther's commentary on Romans:

> While he was describing the change which God works in the heart through faith in Christ, I felt my heart strangely warmed. I felt I did trust in Christ, Christ alone for salvation; and an assurance was given me that He had taken away my sins, even mine, and saved me from the law of sin and death.[7]

Both Bunyan and Wesley credited their conversions to Luther's explanation of the gospel as he expounded the Word of God. They, in turn, would later bring the gospel to untold numbers.

Luther began the Reformation. Already in his lifetime, the Protestant movement shattered into a multitude of theologies, with Luther's being one of them. It is commonly said that Luther did not carry the Reformation far enough, that he clung to many medieval practices and beliefs, such as the high view of the sacraments, and that the

Reformation of the church had to be completed by others. Some, however, would argue that the alleged medieval holdovers were actually due to Luther's biblicism.

Of the two great theologians of the Reformation, it has been observed that John Calvin developed his thought in a monumental work of systematic theology, *The Institutes*. Luther, on the other hand, developed his thought in commentaries on the Bible.[8]

One can certainly make the case that we need systematic theology, and the Lutherans would develop systematicians of their own, such as Chemnitz. But Luther's method was to hew as closely as he could to the contours of Scripture. Again, he reflected deeply on the Word of God, but he mistrusted reliance on human reason when it came to interpreting Scripture.

What many object to in Luther's theology is often his stubborn insistence on following the Word of God wherever it leads. Luther had a high view of the Lord's Supper. He also had a high view of baptism, taking the texts about how those who have been baptized have put on Christ (Galatians 3:27) and have been buried with Christ (Romans 6:3–4) in dead earnest. But surely it is faith that saves. Of course, Luther would say, so baptism bestows faith and it is one of those objective works of Christ to which our faith clings. Why do you baptize infants? Infants too can be buried into Christ, and they too can have faith, which is not to be confused with intellectual knowledge.

Luther affirmed the Bible texts that speak of our eternal security, *and* he affirmed the Bible texts that warn Christians lest they fall. Calvin would affirm the former and explain away the latter. Arminius would stress how we can fall away and say that the texts about assurance have a restricted meaning. Luther would insist on the assurance texts to someone who was despairing of his sins and doubting his salvation; he would insist on the warning texts to someone who was complacent and living an immoral life. One text is law, designed to terrify and bring to repentance; the other is gospel, designed to comfort and save. An ordinary person might say, "Which is it? Can I lose my salvation or not?" Luther would accuse that person of appealing to human reason instead of to God's Word, which applies to his spiritual needs in a complex and dynamic way.

Again, theologians of other traditions will insist that we need to apply reason to tie together the truths of Scripture and that we need to figure out one definite answer to the various questions we have. Luther refused to play that game.

Luther kept much of the old liturgy because it consisted of quotations of the Word of God, and what better way is there to worship God than with His Word? He believed that the Word was primarily the liberating gospel, so he did not turn the Bible into just a rule book or a moral manual. He saw the Word of God, which when connected to the physical elements makes the sacraments, as a means of grace through which the Holy Spirit brings us to Christ.

Many Christians will not follow Luther all the way into all of his theology. But here are some elements that virtually all of the traditions who followed after him take for granted and owe to Luther: the Bible as the highest authority; the right of laypeople to read the Bible; having a

Bible in your own language; having been taught to read so that you can read the Bible in your own language.

This is not all. Congregational singing is something that did not really exist in the church before Luther. So if you sing in church, that is part of Luther's legacy.

If you celebrate Christmas, you owe a debt to Luther, whose Christmas sermons, carols, and writings did much to humanize the Christ child—who before was portrayed like a little judge—and His mother, whom Luther honored not by making her into the queen of heaven but by celebrating the faith of a young peasant girl. It is said that Luther started the custom of the Christmas tree. Many modern scholars doubt that now, but it could have happened. Whether he did or not, that there is a legend to that effect points to the role people recognized Luther played, of turning a day formerly devoted to rituals and reveling into a joyful family day, bringing symbols of everlasting life into the home, and putting the Christ of Scripture back into the holiday.

The Christian family, though not of course invented by Luther, was nevertheless part of his legacy. Before Luther, those who wanted to be truly spiritual rejected marriage and having children as being worldly, choosing instead the supposedly higher calling of the monastery, the convent, or the priest's cell. Luther, though, stressed marriage and parenthood as among the highest Christian callings. Before Luther, many marriages and the approach to parenthood *were* worldly, with both wives and children often treated like mere possessions.

Luther and Katie, in their very public household, modeled the loving relationship between husband and wife and the loving relationship between parents and children. The spiritual exercises that took place in a legalistic way in the monasteries and convents were transformed by the gospel and brought into the home, with family devotions, the father catechizing his children, the whole family singing hymns together, and Bible reading. Luther brought out the spirituality of the home.

His Cultural Legacy

*L*UTHER'S THEOLOGY MEANT THAT laypeople should read the Bible. Late medieval society was mostly illiterate. So the churches of the Reformation opened schools. Ordinary people learned to read the Bible. But once they could read the Bible, they were no longer illiterate, and the whole world was opened up to the average peasant.

It was also significant that those schools opened by the Reformers followed, at Luther's urging, a curriculum designed by Melanchthon, who, in addition to his work as a theologian, was one of the greatest classical scholars. He saw that the schools followed a classical, liberal arts curriculum. The "liberal" comes from the Latin word for freedom, the idea being that in the Greek democracies and the Roman republic, free citizens needed a much different kind of education than the manual training given to slaves. They needed one that developed the mind and the imagination to equip free people to rule themselves. Throughout the Reformation lands—and later even the Counter-Reformation lands—the people on the bottom rung of the feudal hierarchy were getting an education that equipped them for freedom.

These newly educated peasants also had a new work ethic, inspired by Luther's doctrine of vocation. Work had a new meaning and a new value. Seeing one's work as a sacred calling, seeing one's talents as a unique gift of God, and seeing the workplace as an arena for Christian service meant that ordinary craftsmen and laborers poured themselves into their work in a newly energized way. These hard-working, newly educated peasants, some of whom started businesses that earned them great wealth, soon found themselves in the middle class.

It took awhile, of course, for the middle class to become dominant. Something else that would help was the Thirty Years' War, the final attempt by the Catholic Church to put down Protestantism by force, a nightmarish bloodbath from 1618 to 1648 that by some accounts wiped out nearly a third of the population of Germany. The unintended consequences of this tragic religious war was to create a huge labor shortage, which meant that workers could demand more money for their labor, and massive displacements of the population, which meant that peasants were no longer irrevocably tied to the land as they were under the feudal system. Many moved into the cities and otherwise began new lives.

Eventually, the new middle class—now educated, holding property, and often wealthier than the declining aristocracy—demanded a say in their own government. Parliaments that had their origin in the Middle Ages became more powerful over and against the medieval monarchs. In England, the House of Commons—which consisted mostly of Reformation-minded Puritans—went so far as to execute their king, set up a republic for a while, and then reestablish the monarchy, though periodically changing the dynasties.

Meanwhile, the humanist tradition created absolute monarchs mostly in Catholic lands such as Spain and France. Humanism also sparked the Enlightenment, which generated new forms of absolutist governments such as the Reign of Terror and Napoleon in France, Frederick the Great of Prussia, communism, fascism, and other utopian schemes designed by human reason that neglect the reality of human sin. Full political freedom was not won in Europe until the latter half of the twentieth century.

But in America the settlers were Reformation saturated, with many of them coming here to either flee religious persecution or simply to practice their faith unhindered by a meddling state church. The American settlers included large numbers of Lutherans who left their homelands because their princes were imposing a non-Lutheran religion. In Europe the development of the state church conflicted profoundly with Luther's doctrine of the two kingdoms and would lead to a politicization and a liberalization of the church that would have appalled Luther. In America, though, the separation of church and state—in its *proper* sense, in which God is recognized as the ultimate authority in both spheres—embodies Luther's understanding better than in any of the Lutheran states in Europe.

Something needs to be said about those who say that Luther's legacy was the rise of Nazism. That was the thesis of World War II historian William Shirer, and it has been enshrined and popularized in the Holocaust Museum in Washington DC. The contention is that Luther's harsh writing against the Jews and his insistence that Christians should submit to the ruling authorities shaped German culture so that it embraced Adolf Hitler. This charge has been ably refuted by Uwe Siemon-Netto in his brilliant book *The Fabricated Luther.*[9]

The fact is, as we have seen, Luther's ideas brought resistance to authority everywhere they went, often to the Reformer's chagrin, but he himself is the model for the one man who dared to defy both pope and emperor, both the highest religious and political authorities, when he became convinced they were the ones rebelling against the Word of God. As for the Nazis, Hitler hated Christianity. While he paid grudging respect to his native Catholicism for its authoritarianism, he hated Protestantism, which he considered essentially "Jewish" for its reliance on the Hebrew Scriptures, which infected Western civilization, in his mind, with "Jewish" notions such as monotheism, the demystification of nature, and an objective, transcendent morality.

While the liberal state Protestant church, which by then had become an ecumenical hybrid dominated by anti-Jewish higher critics of the Bible, was indeed Nazified—to the point of voting to remove the Old Testament from the Bible—the Christians who agreed with the theology of Luther, along with Calvinists, formed the underground "confessing church," rallying around the Reformation confessions. Lutheran theologians such as Dietrich Bonhoeffer and Herman Sasse opposed Nazism, with Bonhoeffer and others giving their lives for their faith.

As for Hitler, who did try to exploit Luther as an icon of the German people, he was in reality the Anti-Luther. Followers went so far as to publish Hitler's *Table Talk*. But he summed up his beliefs in his great propaganda film *The Triumph of the Will*, which expresses the Nietzschean belief currently back in vogue among postmodernists that we create our own values and our own truths by the power of our will. The title inverted Luther's *Bondage of the Will*, which recognized the truth demonstrated by Hitler, that since our wills are in bondage to sin, when we give them free rein, the result will be unimaginable evil.[10]

Marxists paid Luther the backhanded compliment of having initiated the bourgeois revolution. The communists, who after World War II would rule Wittenberg and the other Lutheran lands of East Germany, actually preserved and honored the Luther sites. In the Marxist world view, history consists of class struggles punctuated by key revolutions. Luther was a catalyst in the revolution against the feudal system, which overthrew the medieval economic and political system of aristocrats dominating the peasants and living off their labor. After that revolution, the middle class reigned. The communists, of course, dismissed the religious issues and interpreted Luther as the embodiment of vast social and economic forces. Communism rests on the premise that the middle class must be destroyed, overthrown by the workers who do not own property, so that everything Luther stood for must be liquidated. But still, the Marxists acknowledged his historical importance in the emergence of the middle class. This may be one of the few notions—maybe the only notion—in which the Marxists were correct.

Luther's impact on the formation of the middle class went beyond economics and social mobility. The ideal of the "middle class family"—so derided by today's leftists and the cultural avant garde—with the father, mother, and children all living together in a happy home, owes much to Luther's writings and his example.

Individualism is another much-derided middle-class value, but this too owes much to Luther. That an individual has direct access to God, apart from the mediating institutions of a church hierarchy, would have monumental implications for Western culture. This view, Luther would certainly say, was taken to extreme by some who followed in his train. It was never his intention that individuals would interpret the Bible for themselves in the sense of making up their own private theologies. Nor was it his intention to create the impression that individuals do not need the church. They need the church precisely to teach and proclaim and apply the Word of God. Radical religious individualism can end up replacing the Word of God with a private, personal subjectivism. Luther was all about what he came to refer to as the "external Word," not individualism as such. But his insistence that the Word addresses individuals *personally,* making possible a *personal* relationship with Christ, was of monumental importance.

Luther's own self-searching, the intense psychological honesty of his writings, and his insistence that all Christians should see the spiritual significance of their sufferings, their inner struggles, and their relationship with God opened up a new attention to the inner life.

Other elements of individualism were also valued in the wake of Luther's example, elements that in other societies are looked down upon. In the West, we appreciate strong, colorful, unique personalities. We appreciate nonconformists over those who always follow the crowd. We appreciate someone who stands alone.

One Little Word

*J*UST AS I AM writing this, the first collection of Luther's music was released as a recording, a boxed set consisting of four CDs. It is remarkable that this has never been done before, as is the fact that less than half of Luther's writings are available in English, suggesting that Luther's influence may not be over.

The collection, *Martin Luther: Hymns, Ballads, Chants, Truth*, from Concordia Publishing House, has forty-nine songs. Lyrically, in the power of their poetry, and musically, in the beauty and aptness of the melodies, they are stunning. They remind us that Luther was also a great artist.

His contributions as a literary artist, of course, are part of his legacy. His rendition of the Bible created a language and a style for the rest of German literature. Classicists say that Luther's Latin style is nearly unsurpassed for his day.[11] His sermons and his other writings, in their imagery, expressiveness, and communicative power, are works of art in themselves.

But Luther's artistry—in which his inmost feelings and convictions are best expressed—is found above all in his music, which gave the greatest of all Lutheran artists, Johann Sebastian Bach, material to work with, and which generations have counted as among their favorite hymns.

The most beloved of them all, of course, finding its way into the hymnbooks of every Christian tradition—including now even those of Roman Catholics—is "A Mighty Fortress Is Our God." It was probably written in the late 1520s while Luther was in the middle of the Sacramentarian conflict, beleaguered on every side, the fate of the Reformation and his own life very much in doubt.

The song is about spiritual conflict. It is filled with the imagery of medieval warfare: castle, shield, a prince, a kingdom. It also has to do with the medieval practice of the champion. In the primitive trials by combat, disputes and charges were sometimes settled by having the two disputants fight to see whom God would allow to win. A weak contestant might find a champion. This was a knight who would fight on his behalf.

In this great hymn, the battle is with the devil. "Deep guile and great might are his dread arms in fight." We cannot defeat him. "On earth is not his equal."[12] Our strength is nothing to his. "With might of ours can naught be done." But we have a champion.

"For us fights the valiant one." Jesus Christ. He is the Lord of hosts. There is no other God. "He holds the field forever." And what is His weapon that defeats the devil, that renders him harmless, that means we no longer need to tremble or fear? The Word of God.

"This world's prince [that is, the devil] may scowl fierce as he will, but "he's judged; the deed is done. One little word can fell him."

Though we may still suffer in this world, though our family, our possessions, our life may yet be taken from us, Christ is "by our side upon the plain / With His good gifts and Spirit." Christ is our mighty fortress, our shield, and our weapon. No matter what anyone can do to us, we have His kingdom.

That "little word" of God gave Luther his place to stand. And with that little word, he moved the world.

THE LESSONS OF LEADERSHIP

~ A leader knows the power of words.

~ A leader recognizes that he is a sinner.

~ A Christian leader recognizes that he is also a saint.

~ Leadership is a calling.

~ A leader bears the cross.

~ A Christian leader trusts that God is in control.

~ A leader is likable.

~ A leader has a sense of perspective.

~ A leader has patience.

~ A leader is willing to go beyond pragmatism.

~ A leader is willing to stand alone.

~ A leader has boldness.

~ A leader is open.

~ Christian leadership requires prayer.

~ Christian leadership requires meditation on the Word of God.

ᑌ Christian leaders face trials.

ᑌ Leaders can ignore their own self-interest.

ᑌ Leaders dislike chaos.

ᑌ Leaders can be angry.

ᑌ A good leader is generous, even to his adversaries.

ᑌ A good leader is not snobbish or elitist but respects ordinary people.

ᑌ A Christian leader remembers his other callings.

ᑌ A good leader can accept paradox.

ᑌ Christian leaders battle the devil.

ᑌ Effective leaders have a sense of humor.

ᑌ A good leader can be immovable.

ᑌ A Christian leader knows the freedom of the gospel.

ᑌ A Christian leader trusts Scripture.

ᑌ A Christian leader clings to Christ.

ᑌ A Christian leader dies in the faith.

NOTES

BIBLIOGRAPHY

INDEX

NOTES

1. This discussion of the Archimedean paradox, including the failures of humanism and Luther's having overcome the dilemma, is drawn from John Carroll, *Humanism: The Wreck of Western Culture* (London: Fontana, 1993), 2–7.
2. The *Life* magazine list can be found at http://www.life.com/Life /millennium/people/01.html.
3. The Canadian list can be found at http://www.adherents.com/ largecom/influ_mil100.html.
4. Agnes Hooper Gottlieb et al., *1,000 Years, 1,000 People: Ranking the Men and Women Who Shaped the Millennium* (Tokyo: Kodansha International, 1998).

PART 1: THE LIFE OF MARTIN LUTHER

1. Quoted in Martin Brecht, *Martin Luther: His Road to Reformation, 1483–1521,* trans. James L. Schaaf (Minneapolis: Fortress, 1985), 13.
2. A good description of this spiritual state can be found in Werner Elert, *The Structure of Lutheranism* (St. Louis: Concordia, 1962), 17–58, under the heading "The Wrath of God."
3. John Milton, "Areopagitica," in *The Student's Milton,* ed. Frank Patterson (New York: Appleton-Century-Crofts, 1957), 741.
4. Brecht, *Road to Reformation,* 125.
5. There is a scholarly legend (something more like an urban legend) that Luther's insight into the gospel came while he was on the privy. Brecht recounts the story and why it is not true. Luther did say that it happened "in the tower." That tower was called the

cloaca tower (i.e., "privy tower," since that was where the monastery's facilities were situated]. But that was not the only room contained in the tower. The third floor had a heated study room that Luther used. See ibid., 227.

6. Martin Luther, "Preface to the Complete Edition of Luther's Latin Writings" (1545), in *Martin Luther: Selections from His Writings*, ed. John Dillenberger (New York: Anchor Books, 1961), 11.

7. Ibid.

8. I am indebted to John Kleinig for this formulation in a lecture he delivered at Elm Grove Lutheran Church, Elm Grove, Wisconsin.

9. Brecht, *Road to Reformation*, 236.

10. Ibid., 230.

11. Hajo Holborn, *A History of Modern Germany: The Reformation* (Princeton, NJ: Princeton University Press, 1982), 44. Thanks to Jason Grimes and the Arador Armour Library Web site for the reference.

12. Brecht, *Road to Reformation*, 182.

13. See Thesis 75, *Selections from His Writings*, 498.

14. Luther, "The Ninety-Five Theses," *Selections from His Writings*, 490.

15. Ibid., 493.

16. Ibid.

17. Ibid., 498.

18. Ibid., 495.

19. Ibid.

20. Ibid., 494.

21. Ibid., 496.

22. Brecht, *Road to Reformation*, 210.

23. Ibid., 206.

24. M. Stanton Evans, *The Theme Is Freedom: Religion, Politics, and the American Tradition* (Washington DC: Regnery, 1996).

25. Quoted in Brecht, *Road to Reformation*, 251.

26. Quoted in ibid., 420.

27. Luther, *Selections from His Writings*, 500.

28. See Alister E. McGrath, *Luther's Theology of the Cross: Martin Luther's Theological Breakthrough* (Oxford and New York: Basil

Blackwell, 1985). See also Gene Veith, *Spirituality of the Cross: The Way of the First Evangelicals* (St. Louis: Concordia, 1999).

29. Quoted in Brecht, *Road to Reformation,* 313.

30. Martin Luther, "The Freedom of a Christian," in *Selections from His Writings,* 52.

31. Ibid., 66.

32. Ibid., 76.

33. Ibid.

34. Quoted in Lewis Spitz, *The Protestant Reformation, 1517–1559* (St. Louis: Concordia, 2001), 84. There are different accounts of the exact wording based on various transcripts of the diet. The "Here I stand" phrase is not in the official record, but contemporary witnesses record it. Philip Schaff discusses this at some length, concluding that the words were extemporaneous, in German, after Eck's interruption. Some accounts say that after "Here I stand," Luther said, "I can do no other" (*Ich kann nicht anders*), but Schaff could not find that phrase in the earliest sources. See Schaff, *The German Reformation,* vol. 7, *History of the Christian Church* (New York: Scribner's, 1914), 305n, 309–10.

35. Spitz, *Protestant Reformation,* 84; cf. Brecht, *Road to Reformation,* 461.

36. Schaff, *German Reformation,* 345.

37. See Schaff's discussion of the influence of Luther's Bible on the German language and on German literature, ibid., 357–59.

38. Ibid., 350.

39. Ibid., 376–77.

40. Ibid., 378.

41. Ibid., 380.

42. Quoted in ibid., 389.

43. Luther wrote a book on the subject, *Against the Heavenly Prophets in the Matter of Images and Sacraments* (1535). For further discussion of the Reformers' views on the arts—and how even John Calvin and Ulrich Zwingli were not anti-art—and how these views shaped the art that emerged under their influence, see Gene Veith, *Painters of Faith: The Spiritual Landscape in Nineteenth-Century America* (Washington DC: Regnery, 2001), 9–24.

44. Spitz, *Protestant Reformation,* 118, 166–67.

45. Ibid., 126–28.

46. Ibid., 128–30.

47. Quoted in Martin Brecht, *Martin Luther: Shaping and Defining the Reformation, 1521–1532,* trans. James L. Schaaf (Minneapolis: Fortress, 1994), 103.

48. Quoted in ibid., 104.

49. Rudolf K. Markwald and Marilyn Morris Marwald, *Katharina Von Bora, A Reformation Life* (St. Louis: Concordia, 2002), 42–43. The information in this section is drawn from this delightful book.

50. Quoted in ibid., 63.

51. Ibid.

52. Ibid., 70, from a letter of Luther's.

53. Ibid., 77.

54. Quoted in Martin Brecht, *Martin Luther: The Preservation of the Church,* trans. James L. Schaaf (Minneapolis: Fortress, 1999), 20.

55. Quoted in Markwald and Markwald, *Katharina Von Bora,* 98.

56. Ibid., 137.

57. Ibid., 139–40.

58. Quoted in Schaff, *German Reformation,* 443.

59. See ibid., 444–45, and Spitz, *Protestant Reformation,* 108–9.

60. Quoted in Schaff, *German Reformation,* 445.

61. Quoted in Brecht, *Shaping and Defining the Reformation,* 180.

62. Schaff, *German Reformation,* 447.

63. Ibid. Spitz, *Protestant Reformation,* 111, believes that number is exaggerated since that would have decimated the princes' labor force.

64. Schaff, *German Reformation,* 447–48.

65. Martin Luther, *Dr. Martin Luther's Small Catechism* (St. Louis: Concordia, 1943), 5.

66. Ibid., 6.

67. Ibid., 10.

68. Schaff, *German Reformation,* 502.

69. Don Nevile, "Martin Luther Caught in the Pub?" *Adoramus* (September 2001), see http://www.albertasynod.ca/resources/worship/adoramus/20010900.html#luther.

70. My translation of *Ihr habt einen anderen Geist als wir.* See also Schaff, *German Reformation,* 644n.
71. "Evangelical" continued to be the term for Lutherans in Europe. Americans in that tradition still speak of the Evangelical Lutheran Church. The term was subsequently adopted by a wide variety of other groups, being used today to describe the range of conservative Christians who believe in the gospel and in the Scriptures.
72. For the challenge of Islam to the West and Luther's response, see Gene Veith, *Christianity in an Age of Terrorism* (St. Louis: Concordia, 2002).
73. *On War Against the Turk* (1529); *A Sermon Against the Turks* (1529); *The Preface to a Book on Life and Customs of the Turks by George von Muhlbach* (1530); *Appeal to Prayer Against the Turks* (1541); *Refutation of the Qur'an* (1542, a book by Recaldo da Montecroce with Luther's preface and additional material); and the preface to Theodor Bibliander's Latin translation of the Koran (1543), which was published at Luther's urging.
74. The siege began on September 23, 1529. One hundred thousand Turks surrounded the city, which was garrisoned by twenty thousand Viennese soldiers. The Turks withdrew after twenty-five days.
75. Schaff, *German Reformation,* 698.
76. Ibid., 699.
77. Brecht, *Preservation of the Church,* 229.
78. See Brecht's summary of the book in *Shaping and Defining the Reformation,* 112–13.
79. Quoted in Brecht, *Preservation of the Church,* 349.
80. Ibid., 372.
81. Ibid., 373.
82. Ibid., 375.
83. Ibid., 376. The account of Luther's death is based on Brecht.

Part 2: The Character of Martin Luther

1. Quoted in Brecht, *Martin Luther: Shaping and Defining the Reformation, 1521–1532,* trans. James L. Schaaf (Minneapolis: Fortress, 1994), 330.

2. See Gustav Wingren, *Luther on Vocation* (Evansville, IN: Ballast, 1994). See also Gene Veith, *God at Work: Your Christian Vocation in All of Life* (Wheaton, IL: Crossway, 2002).

3. See Alister E. McGrath, *Luther's Theology of the Cross: Martin Luther's Theological Breakthrough* (Oxford and New York: Basil Blackwell, 1985), and Veith, *Spirituality of the Cross.*

4. Quoted in Philip Schaff, *The German Reformation,* vol. 7, *History of the Christian Church* (New York: Scribner's, 1914), 389.

5. Ewald M. Plass, ed., *What Luther Says* (St. Louis: Concordia, 1959), 351.

6. Ibid., 351–52.

7. Martin Luther, *Works,* ed. Jaroslav Pelikan and Helmut Lehman, 55 vols. (St. Louis: Concordia; Philadelphia: Fortress, 1958–86) 48:281–82.

8. Brecht, *Shaping and Defining the Reformation,* 397.

9. Ibid.

10. Plass, *What Luther Says,* 1094.

11. Ibid., 1093.

12. Ibid., 1095.

13. Ibid., 1360.

14. Ibid., 83.

15. Ibid., 79.

16. Ibid., 1380–81.

17. Ibid., 28–29.

18. Quoted in Rudolf K. Markwald and Marilyn Morris Marwald, *Katharina Von Bora, A Reformation Life* (St. Louis: Concordia, 2002), 135.

19. Plass, *What Luther Says,* 29.

20. Roland Bainton, *Here I Stand: A Life of Martin Luther* (Nashville, TN: Abingdon, 1978), 229.

21. Markwald and Markwald, *Katharina Von Bora,* 87.

22. Bainton, *Here I Stand,* 229.

23. Plass, *What Luther Says,* 1086.

24. Ibid., 142.

25. Ibid., 142–43.

26. Quoted in Markwald and Markwald, *Katharina Von Bora,* 94–95.

27. Schaff, *German Reformation,* 335.
28. Ibid., 336.
39. Plass, *What Luther Says,* 403.
30. Ibid., 396.
31. My translation, from the German quoted in Schaff, *German Reformation,* 335.
32. Bainton, *Here I Stand,* 231–33.
33. Ibid., 232.
34. Plass, *What Luther Says,* 776–77.
35. Ibid., 777.
36. Ibid.
37. Ibid., 87.
38. "Large Catechism," IV. 57, in *The Book of Concord: The Confessions of the Evangelical Lutheran Church,* trans. Theodore G. Tappert (Philadelphia: Fortress, 1959), 444.
39. Plass, *What Luther Says,* 90.
40. Ibid.
41. Ibid., 368.
42. Ibid., 366–67.
43. Ibid., 372.
44. Ibid., 374.
45. Ibid.

PART 3: THE LEGACY OF MARTIN LUTHER

1. Lewis Spitz, *The Protestant Reformation, 1517–1559* (St. Louis: Concordia, 2001), 124.
2. Ibid., 117.
3. Ibid., 125.
4. Quoted in Rudolf K. Markwald and Marilyn Morris Marwald, *Katharina Von Bora, A Reformation Life* (St. Louis: Concordia, 2002), 192.
5. Concordia Publishing House has recently announced a project to translate the rest of Luther's works into English.
6. John Bunyan, *Grace Abounding to the Chief of Sinners* (London: Religious Tract Society, 1905), see http://www.gutenberg.net/etext/654.

7. Wesley, *Journal*, May 24, 1738, see http://www.gospelcom.net /chi/DAILYF/2001/05/daily-05-24-2001.shtml.

8. The point was made by Robert Minor, professor of religious studies at the University of Kansas.

9. Uwe Siemon-Netto, *The Fabricated Luther* (St. Louis: Concordia, 1995).

10. See Gene Veith, *Modern Fascism: Liquidating the Judeo-Christian Worldview* (St. Louis: Concordia, 1993).

11. So E. Christian Kopff, Latin professor at the University of Colorado, tells me.

12. I am following the translation in the book accompanying the boxed set of CDs, *Martin Luther: Hymns, Ballads, Chants, Truth* (St. Louis: Concordia, 2004), 61–62.

BIBLIOGRAPHY

Bainton, Roland. *Here I Stand: A Life of Martin Luther.* Nashville, TN: Abingdon, 1978.

Book of Concord: The Confessions of the Evangelical Lutheran Church. Translated by Theodore G. Tappert. Philadelphia: Fortress, 1959.

Brecht, Martin. *Martin Luther: Shaping and Defining the Reformation, 1521–1532.* Translated by James L. Schaaf. Minneapolis: Fortress, 1994.

———. *Martin Luther: His Road to Reformation, 1483–1521.* Translated by James L. Schaaf. Minneapolis: Fortress, 1985.

———. *Martin Luther: The Preservation of the Church.* Translated by James L. Schaaf. Minneapolis: Fortress, 1999.

Bunyan, John. *Grace Abounding to the Chief of Sinners.* London: Religious Tract Society, 1905. See http://www.gutenberg.net/etext/654.

Carroll, John. *Humanism: The Wreck of Western Culture.* London: Fontana, 1993.

Elert, Werner. *The Structure of Lutheranism.* St. Louis: Concordia, 1962.

Evans, M. Stanton. *The Theme Is Freedom: Religion, Politics, and the American Tradition.* Washington DC: Regnery, 1996.

Gottlieb, Agnes Hooper et al. *1,000 Years, 1,000 People: Ranking the Men and Women Who Shaped the Millennium.* Tokyo: Kodansha International, 1998.

Holborn, Hajo. *A History of Modern Germany: The Reformation.* Princeton, NJ: Princeton University Press, 1982.

Luther, Martin. *Dr. Martin Luther's Small Catechism.* St. Louis: Concordia, 1943.

———. *Hymns, Ballads, Chants, Truth.* St. Louis: Concordia, 2004. 3-CD boxed set.

———. *Works.* Edited by Jaroslav Pelikan and Helmut Lehman. 55 vols. St. Louis: Concordia; Philadelphia: Fortress, 1958–86.

———. *Selections from His Writings.* Edited by John Dillenberger. New York: Anchor Books, 1961.

Markwald, Rudolf K., and Marilyn Morris Marwald. *Katharina Von Bora: A Reformation Life.* St. Louis: Concordia, 2002.

McGrath, Alister E. *Luther's Theology of the Cross: Martin Luther's Theological Breakthrough.* Oxford and New York: Basil Blackwell, 1985.

Nevile, Don. "Martin Luther Caught in the Pub?" *Adoramus* (September 2001). See http://www.albertasynod.ca/resources/worship/adoramus/20010900.html#luther.

Patterson, Frank Allen, ed. *The Student's Milton.* New York: Appleton-Century-Crofts, 1957.

Plass, Ewald M., ed. *What Luther Says.* St. Louis: Concordia, 1959.

Schaff, Philip. *The German Reformation. Vol. 7, History of the Christian Church.* New York: Scribner's, 1914.

Siemon-Netto, Uwe. *The Fabricated Luther.* St. Louis: Concordia, 1995.

Spitz, Lewis. *The Protestant Reformation: 1517–1559.* St. Louis: Concordia, 2001.

Veith, Gene. *God at Work: Your Christian Vocation in All of Life.* Wheaton, IL: Crossway, 2002.

———. *Modern Fascism: Liquidating the Judeo-Christian Worldview.* St. Louis: Concordia, 1993.

———. *Painters of Faith: The Spiritual Landscape in Nineteenth-Century America.* Washington DC: Regnery, 2001.

———. *Spirituality of the Cross: The Way of the First Evangelicals.* St. Louis: Concordia, 1999.

Wesley, John. *Journal.* See http://www.gospelcom.net/chi/DAILYF/2001/05/daily-05-24-2001.shtml.

Wingren, Gustav. *Luther on Vocation.* Evansville, IN: Ballast, 1994.

Index

Printed in the USA
CPSIA information can be obtained
at www.ICGtesting.com
JSHW021955150824
68134JS00046B/1

9 781581 824209